Deeksha

From Karen
8-13-19

Deeksha

The Fire from Heaven

Kiara Windrider with Grace Sears

INNER OCEAN PUBLISHING
Maui • San Francisco

Inner Ocean Publishing, Inc.
P.O. Box 1239
Makawao, Maui, HI 96768-1239
www.innerocean.com

Cover design by Suzanne Albertson
Book design by Madonna Gauding

Inner Ocean Publishing is a member of the Green Press Initiative, a nonprofit program dedicated
to supporting publishers in their efforts to reduce their use of fiber sourced from endangered
forests. We elected to print this title on 50 percent postconsumer recycled paper, with the recycled portion processed free of chlorine. As a result, we have saved the following resources: 33
trees, 14,120 gallons of water, and 5,679 kilowatt-hours of electricity. We have also avoided making 1,557 pounds of solid waste and 3,058 pounds of greenhouse gases. For more information on
the Green Press Initiative, visit www.greenpressinitiative.org.

PUBLISHER CATALOGING-IN-PUBLICATION DATA

Windrider, Kiara.
Deeksha : the fire from heaven / Kiara Windrider with Grace Sears.
-- Maui : Inner Ocean, 2006, c2005.
p. ; cm.
ISBN-13: 978-1-930722-70-5
ISBN-10: 1-930722-70-2
Originally published: Kadugudi, Bangalore : Sal Towers Publishing, 2005.
Includes bibliographical references.
1. Spirituality. 2. Enlightenment (Buddhism) I. Sears, Grace.
II. Title.
BQ935 .W56 2006
294.3/442--dc22 0609

Printed in the United States of America
05 06 07 08 09 10 DATA 10 9 8 7 6 5 4 3 2 1

DISTRIBUTED BY PUBLISHERS GROUP WEST
For information on promotions, bulk purchases, premiums, or educational use, please contact:
866.731.2216 or sales@innerocean.com.

Contents

Foreword

By Members of the Golden Age Foundation

If you have ever been curious about mystics and mysticism, this book is for you. This book is the story of a man who was taken to where we all want to be.

When Kiara was with us at Oneness University, his insatiable thirst for wisdom and his willingness to learn from everyone made him stand apart from the crowd. His unique life experiences and his multifaceted cultural background make him the chosen author of this book.

Kiara expresses his innermost thoughts in this book with utter simplicity and stunning authenticity. His book inspires readers to consider the possibility of their own enlightenment without frightening them, as might the austere and trial-filled path of the great sages and saints. He sends out his clarion call to all humanity, announcing the incredible phenomenon of Amma and Bhagavan, who bestow the state of oneness on all those who seek.

It brings to light the truth of Bhagavan's statement: "Man cannot make it on his own; it has to be given to him." Given it was to Kiara.

The book also is a treasure trove of the insightful teachings of Sri Bhagavan. It will leave every reader astounded at the divine grace of Amma and Bhagavan at work, landing humanity with effortless ease into the cherished state of oneness. A journey that would otherwise take several lifetimes and much travail, happening with such speed and ease in such a short period, leaves the reader wondering at the sheer magic of the *deekshas*. Kiara's narrative is a testimony to this wonder.

When the book was read out loud, Sri Bhagavan remarked that the book itself could serve as a deeksha to those who read it. This book does not require application. Instead, it shows you the futility of effort and awakens you to the power of God.

Author's Note

Deeksha is not so much about experiencing spiritual highs or altered states of consciousness: Instead, it is about bringing these higher realms of awareness all the way into the physical body. As such, you should expect that there could be physical and psychological changes that take place in response to the deeksha, perhaps even from merely reading this book. As the physical body begins to integrate these new energies, some people report headaches, aches and pains in the body, heart palpitations, feelings of disorientation, dizziness, nausea, changes in sleep and eating patterns, hot and cold flashes, flulike symptoms, and so on. There could also be psychological responses as suppressed emotions begin to surface and release. Many people find that old patterns of defense no longer seem to work, and social masks begin to slip. Although this is emotionally freeing, it might also be somewhat uncomfortable.

The deeksha is a powerful energy, capable of shifting long-established patterns and creating powerful inner transformations. It alters consciousness by activating changes in the neurobiology of the brain. Although there is a divine intelligence guiding this process, people sometimes experience temporary flare-ups of certain symptoms as a deeper integration begins to take place. Those with psychiatric disorders or taking psychiatric medications should be aware of this and monitor the extent of their own participation with the deeksha energy.

If you choose to read this book or receive any deekshas, please understand that you may undergo certain physical and emotional changes as you come into more wholeness on a cellular level. Take care of your body by drinking adequate water and using whatever natural supplements you may be familiar with to facilitate a cellular and emotional detoxification. An ability to work through your own emotional issues, or to find somebody who can help with this, may also be a useful asset.

Please note that I, as an author, have no official affiliation with Oneness University, and am simply reporting my own journey and perspectives. The programs offered at Oneness University are continually changing. If readers choose to attend one of these programs, understand that the current focus may be quite different from what is described in these pages, and people's experiences could be subsequently different also.

For one thing, when I did my program, I was one of a group of seven, and Grace was in a unique program all by herself. In contrast, there could be hundreds of people going through the twenty-one-day program at any given time now. In our time, we were given hands-on deekshas, which were usually quite intense. In contrast, the deekshas today are given etherically, and designed for a relatively gradual transformation of consciousness. Rather than the peaks and crashes that many in our groups experienced, these deekshas are designed to minimize the need for a "dark night," and make the process smoother. There are fewer teachings given now, and there seems to be less of a need to go through an intense emotional process. There also seems to be a shift away from the term "enlightenment" with all the associations and expectations that go with it, to the term "oneness."

It appears that each new group of people makes it easier for each group that comes afterward. There also seems to be a shift away from a purely individual focus to deepening our links with the collective consciousness of humanity. Enlightenment, after all, is the recognition that the individual self is more of an illusion than we had previously realized, and that it is only in the realization of our union with all beings that we find our true place and destiny within the web of life.

For anyone choosing to receive hands-on deekshas, there is a wide network of deeksha givers scattered throughout the world today, who may be contacted through the websites listed in the back of the book. There are also courses being offered through Oneness University in India, which are specifically aimed at people who feel it is their calling to become deeksha givers. Along with Carl Calleman, who has been using the insights of the Mayan calendar to understand the shifting energies on the planet today, I feel that such intentional giving will not be necessary for much longer. The morphogenetic fields of oneness are gradually becoming strong enough that the enlightened state will transfer spontaneously from one person to another like wildfire.

How would you know if you were enlightened? Enlightenment does not have to be a dramatic experience for everybody. In fact, I feel it is too easy to mistake the drama of cosmic highs and psychic experiences for the state of egolessness that is the hallmark of enlightenment. Essentially, it is a shift away from being centered in separation and duality to being centered in oneness. Good questions to ask yourself would be: What motivates my life and behaviors? Do I manifest a greater degree of kindness, emotional sensitivity, and compassion? How do I perceive the world and people around me? Do I exist primarily for myself or in service to the whole? In the state of enlightenment, or oneness, there is a growing sense that your life is not your own, that you simply become a vehicle for divine consciousness to move through, a single cell within the body of humanity and within the web of all life. The question of whether you have achieved enlightenment becomes meaningless, for it is only the separate ego that is so richly invested in the answer.

Many have experienced unmistakable shifts in perception and consciousness as an outcome of the deeksha process. Whether we call this "enlightenment," "oneness," or "waking up from illusion" is not so important. As I discuss later in the book, my own sense is that enlightenment is not a single event so much as a series of awakenings. As we continue to integrate this new consciousness into our hearts and lives, we ultimately move towards the transformation of our physical bodies into bodies of light. All this takes time, and we each have a long way to go before we can claim to be "en-lightened" in this sense of the word.

We are shedding old skins as we move toward a new world. In the words of a beautiful Sufi prayer, "O Great Wave, wipe away . . . wipe away my false face. Awaken from my sleep, O radiant light. Touch me . . . touch me . . . and I am once again beyond the beyond—I am That I Am."

June, 2006

Introduction

W hat do you say after a search that has lasted lifetimes has ended? For me, as for many people, enlightenment had always been a destination at the end of the road. Whenever someone asked me to define my highest goal in life, I always said, "Enlightenment." I could never see beyond that. I was so attached to the seeking, the questing, the journeying that I couldn't imagine my life any other way. Who would I be if I ever stopped seeking? No wonder it took so long!

Although I craved enlightenment, some part of me also resisted it. Enlightenment is a warrior's path, I realize now. You battle, you struggle, you fight to get there. And when you finally do, you're dead!

Who dies? After enlightenment, I realized that it is only the illusion of a separate self that dies—the little, fixated self, also known as the ego. My ego had been forever searching, urging, comparing, judging, and never allowing itself to be still, because it was afraid that life would pass it by.

What did I know of life before? Even though I had been on a spiritual path for a long time, I was still very much identified with one little fixation in the boundless flow of life that I called me: the me that felt so unworthy sometimes and was always yearning for more, the me that felt so powerless and was always holding onto what it knew, the me that felt so small that it had to force the universe to fit into its own little concepts of it.

This "me" had tried so desperately to control everything! What did I know of the brilliance of life, the endlessly creative rhythms of the universe, which were constantly beating through my heartbeat in every moment of existence? In trying to control my life, I had only succeeded in separating myself from the river that was continuously seeking to carry me home.

How did I come to the end of the search? Near a small village in south India, in a place known as Golden City or Oneness University, there is an avatar named Bhagavan (not to be confused with Osho, who was also referred to as Bhagavan). People call him a *mukti* avatar, and his life mission is to help people achieve enlightenment. He claims that enlightenment is a neurobiological process, and that all it takes is an adjustment in the brain, which then allows the cosmic energies to flow through and dissolve the concept that we carry around of a separately existing self, which is an illusion of perception.

This happens through a process known as the *deeksha,* a transfer of divine energy in which someone who is trained can place his or her hands on your head and allow cosmic energies to channel through. This energy activates a shift in the neural circuitries of the brain, which eventually leads to enlightenment. Although it should not be expected to create instant enlightenment, the activity of the deeksha creates a link with each person's indwelling divinity, and greatly accelerates the process of soul awakening.

As this restructuring begins to happen, people enter into deep states of silence, peace, joy, or cosmic consciousness. At a certain point, they discover that there is no more a reference point called the self. All that remains is the vast ocean of consciousness. The drop dissolves into the ocean, or perhaps, the ocean dissolves into the drop. All concepts about reality and spirituality disappear into the direct experience of their inner divinity. These people then become beacons of light, capable of expressing their soul destinies in the world.

This book not only describes my own journey of enlightenment, and that of a few others who are well known to me, but also holds out the possibility of planetary enlightenment. Thousands have received this state already, and Bhagavan's mission is ultimately to provide the possibility of enlightenment to every human being on this planet.

What the deeksha seems to activate is not a watered-down version of enlightenment, but the same consciousness experienced by Buddha, Christ, and Ramana Maharishi. It is not based on teachings, morality, or effort, but is a gift of grace. Enlightenment is a neurobiological event. It is also a continually deepening process.

There are so many teachings in the world today, so many traditions and practices, but as many seekers have discovered, these in themselves are not enough to produce enlightenment. Yet as a gift of grace transferred through the deeksha, enlightenment can happen to the unsophisticated villager as easily as to the most ardent spiritual seeker, perhaps easier, because the villager is not bogged down by so many expectations and concepts. It is our natural state, the childlike state that Jesus spoke of when he said, "Unless you become as a little child, you cannot enter the Kingdom of Heaven."

Bhagavan does not say that his is the only way to get enlightened, and has little interest in telling people what they should do or not do. He has no interest in creating yet another religion. His sole mission is to facilitate enlightenment for everyone whose souls desire this.

He often refers to himself as a technician, as one who is capable of creating certain neurobiological shifts in the brain in order to produce enlightenment. It is, he says, a "divine operation," and has nothing to do with dogma, belief, or rituals. Although physical proximity can help, this transmission is beyond the limitations of space and time.

Bhagavan's teachings are universal. "I belong to the whole world and all the world's faiths," he asserts. He emphasizes that all religions have their own purpose, and there is no need for conflict among them. He also asserts that enlightenment has nothing to do with religion. The person who is enlightened has a guiding light within. The person who is spiritually mature needs no external moral code. Bhagavan predicts that organized religions will die a natural death after global enlightenment is accomplished.

My intention in this book is to share some of these understandings as simply as possible, without using too many metaphysical concepts, so that it can be relevant to every seeker, and even to those who might consider themselves beyond religious teachings. Ultimately, the only purpose of these teachings is to point out what you already know, and to guide you into the experience itself.

As I share my own experience of receiving enlightenment, it is with the absolute conviction that anybody is capable of receiving this gift as well. And as more and more people become enlightened, the ripples of enlightenment will sweep throughout the entire planet to all people, whether they are on a spiritual path or not, and even whether they believe in the possibility or not. It is, insists Bhagavan, our divine destiny.

There is never an "only way" to anything, including enlightenment. Just because one particular system seems to work, it does not mean that other systems don't. Similarly, enlightenment is not exclusive. If an avatar is able to activate these states, it does not mean that others cannot. As I make clear later in this book, we are all part of a collective avataric energy that is slowly encircling the planet, and we all have distinct and complementary roles to play in this. Enlightenment is happening as a spontaneous global phenomenon today simply because it is time now, because we have prepared for this collectively for long cycles of evolution, no matter what our individual backgrounds or belief systems may be. In no way would I wish to imply that Bhagavan is the only avatar of enlightenment in the world, or that deeksha is the only means.

Something is changing in the consciousness of humanity. We entered the long-awaited Golden Age in 2003, says Bhagavan, and a new biological species with new genetic possibilities is consequently emerging that will be wired to the state of oneness.

As such, the enlightenment spoken about in this book will soon become a normal way of being for everyone on earth, and indeed there are many today who are already experiencing spontaneous awakenings. For those who would like assistance, however, various deeksha programs are offered at Oneness University (the teaching division of Golden City), and also increasingly around the world, by people who have undergone the training to transmit this state.

Indeed, after reading the manuscript for this book, Bhagavan affirmed that these pages themselves could serve as a deeksha. Bhagavan's energy was very strongly present in the writing of this book, and may likewise inspire you as you read through these pages. Most of this book was written in a ten-day period, following a flow of inspiration so strong that I could not humanly stop writing. It is my wish that all who read this book may feel similarly inspired, knowing that the time of your soul's most profound fulfillment is now here.

Later in this book, I share briefly Sri Aurobindo's vision of the "supramental descent." My hope is to provide a larger context for the revolution that is now taking place in human evolution, in which Sri Bhagavan is playing a key role. The final chapter is a conversation with Bhagavan himself, followed by an appendix highlighting various perspectives on the upcoming "shift of the ages," summarized from my earlier book, *Doorway to Eternity: A Guide to Planetary Ascension.* I believe this will be relevant to readers who wish to understand the scientific as well as the mystical basis for our planetary transition into the Golden Age.

Two more appendixes, written in conversation with neuroscientist Christian Opitz, highlight the relationships among enlightenment, deeksha, and the brain from a neurobiological perspective. A glossary of spiritual terms follows.

We are entering an age, whether we call it the Golden Age or Satya Yuga or the Aquarian Age or the Fifth World, where the veils between the spiritual and material worlds are beginning to dissolve. There once was a time when we were born enlightened, and lived in constant awareness of the unity of all things. In the course of time, for reasons that philosophers and theologians can argue endlessly about and don't really matter anymore, we chose to create dense veils among various aspects of ourselves. These veils are held in the subconscious memory as patterns of separation, forgetfulness, limitation, illusion, fear, and so on.

Our genes mutated to align with these subconscious patterns. This, in turn, created pathways within our brains that generated the illusion of a self within each person that existed separate from everything else. When a deeksha is given, these pathways dissolve, and the person begins to experience reality from the perspective of oneness. When enough people experience this shift in perspective that a critical mass is reached, the collective DNA of humanity will change and global enlightenment will occur.

"When the last trumpet sounds," says the apostle Paul (1 Corinthians 15:52), "we will be changed in the twinkling of an eye." Reader, the last trumpet has sounded; and the presence of beings such as Bhagavan in the world today reflects the human thirst to break out of illusion, to unplug from the matrix, and to reconnect with our divine blueprint.

We cannot solve humanity's problems from the same level of consciousness at which they were created. But we can enter a collective state where the problems themselves disappear in the light of an awakened consciousness. *This is happening now.*

It is an exciting time to be alive. Given what I know today, there is no place I would rather be in this entire vast cosmos than right here on earth during this glorious time of awakening. We have waited lifetimes—eons—for this, and despite all the evidence of my outer senses, there is no doubt in my mind or heart that humanity is going to make it!

The entire world is but a dream in the mind of God. This book is the story of this dream, and of humanity's awakening within the dream!

I notice that the guides now prefer to use the term *oneness* when referring to the experience of enlightenment. *Enlightenment* is a loaded term, and tends to create all sorts of concepts and expectations in the mind. *Oneness* simply opens the heart.

A new phenomenon has begun in recent months. Several disciples have entered into states of consciousness where the personal self completely disappears, and the Divine steps through in a highly focused way. It seems that many of the avatars, masters, and divine personalities from every age and tradition are being enabled now to step through these surrendered beings and create a field of Presence, where a deep activity of grace can be initiated for everyone there. Participants in the twenty-one-day program come to sit quietly in this Presence every evening. Very powerfully and yet very subtly, miracles of transformation follow.

Brother Sun

Brother sun, I asked one day,
Don't you ever tire
Of spinning endless circles across the sky?
Rising, then setting,
Eternal mystery of day and night?
He looked at me then,
Gazing softly into my heart,
Filling me deeply with his light.
It is not I that spins through the skies
Creating days and nights, he said.
Here there is only undying light
Of eternal radiance;
All else is your perception.
See me and you shall see yourself;
All shadows are lifted
In noonday light.
Once you have seen,
No longer can you be a little speck
That blows around
Like chaff in the wind,
Separate and alone.
You, too, shall become a sun
Of undying light;
Yes, be a sun unto yourself,
And we shall circle,
Always eternally within each other.

I

My Journey of Enlightenment

I.

The Search

Following the spiritual path is like being on a journey toward a far land, not knowing the way, not sure the destination exists, somehow knowing we are destined to arrive at God, yet aware also that the self that finally arrives is equally destined to disappear. What can I say about this journey, except to affirm that it begins only after it is over? What can I say about the self, except to assert that I understand myself only when "I" am gone? What can I say about discovering God, except to marvel at all the continually changing, infinitely beautiful expressions of God's face, which is also my own face?

Ever since I can remember, I have been fascinated by stories of holy men and women in the mountaintops and forests of India living in enlightened states of divine union. Yogananda Paramahamsa's *Autobiography of a Yogi* was a firm favorite of mine, along with Swami Rama's *Living with the Himalayan Masters.*

I looked at these extraordinary beings with admiration and some envy, recognizing the longing in my heart to achieve a similar state of enlightenment, yet convinced that I did not have the discipline or stamina required to spend years in a cave, hidden away from the world, seeking this most precious of all pearls.

After a while, I gave up hope. I would never be Buddha or Christ or Ramana Maharshi, and they were the only images

I had of what an enlightened person looked like. I would escape into fantasies of becoming enlightened, not just as a personal experience, but as a global awakening. But I always managed to find my way back to "reality," a word I didn't particularly like, because it had nothing to do with what felt real, yet was something I had to deal with if I were to be of any use on earth.

I justified the abandonment of my quest. How could I feel good about entering into some kind of personal nirvana while billions of people were hell-bent on extinction? How could I justify spending years in a solitary cave when the voices of human need were so loud all around me? What kinds of answers made sense in a world where outer reality seemed to be dominated by greed, hunger, manipulation, destruction, and suffering? Besides, I had been told that only a handful of people had achieved this state since the dawn of history, so what chance did I have of being next in line?

Still, the longing in my heart remained, and I tortured myself with the yearning to break free from the limitations I perceived within my own experience of self, all the while knowing that this was an impossible dream. I was not an avatar. I was too lazy and undisciplined to even meditate regularly, so what was I doing on this quixotic quest? My longing fed a vague hope that someday, somehow I would make it, making the emptiness of the moment a little more bearable.

My journey is not so different from that of anyone else, for underneath all of our separate illusions of reality, there is essentially one soul, one mind, one body, and one consciousness. As I share this journey of awakening, you will perhaps see that it is your journey as well. And more than that, it is also the journey of the vast, unified consciousness that is the collective consciousness of this planet.

I begin my story with an incident that jolted me out of my youthful ignorance one beautiful, sunny morning when I was sixteen. I was a student at the Kodai International School in the lushly forested hills of south India. One fine weekend, a group of us were out on one of our favorite hikes along a winding mountain stream that led to a steeply cascading waterfall that dropped hundreds of feet into a gorge below.

We camped overnight near the streambed, and after a quick breakfast the following morning, two of us went ahead of the group down to the waterfalls. Intoxicated by the perfection of the beauty all around us, we decided to climb down the falls as far as we could. We had climbed several hundred feet when my friend lost his hold and fell. I watched him fall in petrified shock, and continued to watch in frozen horror as I lost my own grip and started to fall.

Fingernails torn and bloody from trying to stop my fall, I bounced rapidly down the steep cliffside, realizing that there was nothing more I could do. Soon, I found myself surrendering to the inevitability of death, and strangely enough, a great peace washed over me. I entered a time zone where everything seemed to slow down, and in my next moment of conscious awareness I found myself standing in a pool, waist deep in water on a ledge of rock jutting out from the cliff, with hundreds of feet of cascading water still below us. Amazingly, my friend had also landed in the same pool. We had fallen two hundred feet, and although hurt and dazed, we were inexplicably, gloriously alive! I realized then that there was a purpose to my life, and that I had been kept alive to fulfill that purpose.

In the months and years afterward, I engaged in a fervent search to understand the meaning and purpose of my life. I studied and explored the teachings and practices of just about every world religious tradition. After graduating from high school, I spent several years living and studying in various ashrams in India—Hindu, Buddhist, and Christian.

After a time, I gave up on organized religion, realizing that much of it was embedded in the past, and feeling that I needed to find a path that spoke more directly to our contemporary human condition.

When I was twenty-one, I received a scholarship for a college in the United States. Bethel College is a small college in Kansas, grounded in the Mennonite traditions of peace and justice. Inspired by people such as Gandhi and Martin Luther King Jr., I became increasingly more aware of the political dimensions of Jesus' ministry.

I began to realize that my spirituality had to extend into the marketplace, engaging with the political, social, and economic realities of the world around me, changing not just individuals but also systems, in order to affect not only their spiritual, but also their physical realities. I majored in Peace Studies and International Development and spent some years actively involved in the peace and environmental movements, struggling to create a better world through political activism.

Since my very early years, I had been passionately interested in saving the environment, and in researching alternative, earth-friendly technologies. I had always been distressed by humanity's blindness and greed regarding nature. During college I connected with the Native American path, a path representing oneness with nature, and with the Great Spirit.

I became interested in shamanism, in understanding the spirit that moved through all things, and in speaking directly with Great Spirit through nature and through what the Australian aborigines called the Dreamtime. I yearned to develop the mystical connection with trees, animals, and nature spirits that the indigenous people all over the world seemed to still maintain. Over the years this led me to learn what amounted to a form of "channeling," where I began to attune to the consciousness of nature spirits, angels, ascended masters, and cosmic beings.

During my years in college, I also became fascinated with the insights of quantum mechanics, astrophysics, and biology, exploring questions about the nature of the universe and the evolution of consciousness. My father was a physicist, so I had always had an interest in the natural sciences, but here I began to walk the bridge between science and spirituality. It was exciting to see the underlying unity between them. Each spoke its own language, but they pointed to the same reality, a reality that could not be easily understood except through direct, intuitive experience.

I also became very interested in the relationships between soul, brain, and consciousness. Many enlightened people, such as U. G. Krishnamurthy and Gopi Krishna, were emphasizing that their enlightenment was not a spiritual event, but a biological one, related to an evolutionary shift in the chemistry of the brain, and this intrigued me. I also studied what scientists, such as Valerie Hunt, were saying about the neurobiology of enlightenment, and became intrigued by technologies that could help to change brain states.

At one of the ashrams where I had lived in India, I became interested in the works of Ken Wilber, Stan Grof, and other leaders in the field of transpersonal psychology, which sought to unify spirituality and psychology in the quest to live out the ultimate in human potential. One technique I learned was Holotropic Breathwork, combining intensive breathing with music, which activated each of the seven chakras in the human energy system.

I practiced this for a time, which led to some intense realizations in my psychoenergetic being. I realized that I wanted to spend my life helping people achieving similar states, and so in my midtwenties enrolled in a graduate program at the California Institute for Integral Studies, founded by a disciple of the great Indian yogi Sri Aurobindo. Five years later, I graduated from John F. Kennedy University with a degree in Transpersonal Counseling Psychology.

Along with my graduate program, I was forever taking all kinds of workshops, learning various forms of therapeutic massage and bodywork, doing Enlightenment Intensives and Vipassana meditation retreats, exploring various channeled teachings, interacting with various spiritual teachers, sitting in sweat lodges, participating in Sufi dancing, and generally exploring every form of spiritual teaching to be found under the California sun.

Shortly after I enrolled at the California Institute for Integral Studies, I began to feel a kind of dissolution of the self, as if my subtle bodies were coming into a vast state of union with a Himalayan master whom I had been connecting with, Babaji. For many months I felt that my own sense of identity had dissolved, and I would wake every morning with strong currents of energy coursing through my body. I experienced a state of bliss, accompanied by many realizations about the nature of the universe and human consciousness. After a few months, however, this state faded and eventually disappeared, leaving me with a profound sense of disappointment and failure.

After graduating, I worked for some years as a psychotherapist at an alternative healing center, the Pocket Ranch Institute. It was directed by Barbara Findeisen and Tony Madrid, and their dream was to provide a safe place for people to go through spiritual crisis and kundalini awakening.

Affiliated with the Spiritual Emergence Network, we had various programs for people to release emotional traumas from the past, and to reconnect with their higher selves. The ranch was situated on 3,000 acres of wild oaks, mountain streams, and open meadows, on land that had been held sacred as a place of spiritual visioning for hundreds of years. It was a unique program, and I loved every minute of it.

My home during this time was in Mount Shasta in California; this area was a powerful vortex of sacred energy. I spent a lot of time up in the alpine meadows, communing with the spirits of the mountain, and with the ascended masters, whose presence was so tangible there. It was a beautiful time of discovery, broadening my vision of what our planetary journey was all about. I also spent a lot of time in Hawaii, playing with the dolphins and whales in their ocean world, allowing them to teach me about oneness.

Gradually, I started putting various pieces together that pointed to a world of new possibilities. I studied various calendar systems and prophecies from around the world, I researched little-known scientific findings, I found myself inspired by visions of the future that people were having worldwide, and even encountered aspects of myself from other timelines, all of which pointed to a collective shift in consciousness that awaited humanity in the near future. I wrote a book about all this, *Doorway to Eternity: A Guide to Planetary Ascension*.

What was missing, however, was a plan. It was all very well to say that this was where humanity was headed, and even to feel the truth of this on a very deep level. But then I would read about another round of terrorism in yet another corner of the Earth, whether state-sponsored or otherwise, or hear about another tribe of indigenous people displaced as their forest was destroyed so that yet another corporate entity could profit from the blood of the living Earth.

Was there a point of convergence between my deeply felt inner visions and these fractured outer realities? Or was I simply another casualty of a head-in-the-clouds spirituality that was irrelevant to the outer world?

2.

Meeting Bhagavan

In early 2002 I met a woman who later became my wife. Her name was Grace Sears. Shortly after we met, she had a vision where an ancient being appeared to her in the guise of an Indian woman draped completely in plain white cotton. She revealed herself to be Mother India, and showed her a vast landscape that lay dry and barren under a cloudless sky, with cracks in the ground several inches wide. Only a few people wandered in the distance. "My children are dying," she said. "They need food, they need water, and they need people who care. People must begin to care." Grace remained in that waking vision for an entire day, feeling the pain, parched with heat and thirst, and throwing up repeatedly. She became vast. She was Mother India, and felt her body had become the land. She felt as though she was vomiting up earthquakes for India, so they wouldn't have to be experienced by the land physically.

Inexplicably, after twenty-two years of living in the United States, I, too, began feeling a strong urge to go to India, the land of my birth. As I spoke about this with a trusted friend, Barry, he had the premonition that I would meet somebody who could guide me into the highest states of enlightenment. I felt the truth of his statement as an upwelling of joy throughout my body.

Neither of us knew why or where, but both Grace and I knew we had to go. The call was becoming too strong to ignore. We packed up our bags, put everything into storage, and were on a plane to India by late September.

We traveled through many ashrams, meeting many yogis and gurus. We became attracted to the works of Sri Aurobindo, a freedom fighter, mystic, and highly accomplished yogi who had lived much of his life in contemplation in Pondicherry, India. Joined in this work later by a Frenchwoman, Mirra Alfassa, who eventually came to be known as the Mother, his great task was to anchor into the collective consciousness of humanity what he called the supramental force, a force that would awaken humanity to its true evolutionary destiny as a supramental species, as far beyond the current human species as contemporary humanity is beyond early humans.

Grace and I spent much time in Auroville, the city of human unity founded by the Mother after the death of Sri Aurobindo. We connected with the spirits of these two vision-aries, and had some powerful glimpses of the supramental realms. We spent a lot of time meditating in the Matrimandir, a golden sphere in the center of Auroville, which represented a vehicle for the descent of this supramental force.

One day, as we were meditating in the early dawn, Grace had a visitation from a beautiful, tall, male being, smeared in ash, greenish gray in color, and bare-chested, with some of his hair up in a topknot and some down in dreadlocks. He had strands of beads around his neck.

There was an aura of powerful benevolence about him. He extended his hand to her, holding out a long, luminous oval swirling with a soft green and pink opalescence. She heard the words "cosmic egg." He was so real it seemed she could touch him. She didn't know who he was, but as she described him to me, I realized that this was Shiva. The image remained in her consciousness for weeks, and seemed to be a guiding force as we journeyed along.

In August 2003, we were guided to meet an avatar named Bhagavan. I had been invited to speak at The Experience Festival, a biannual event cosponsored by his Golden Age Foundation and the Global Oneness Foundation, brainchild of two Swedes, Jonas Lindquist and Parlan Fritz. Toward the end of this weeklong event, Grace and I, along with the other teachers and spouses at the event, were invited to have a *darshan* with Bhagavan.

The name *Bhagavan* means "divine avatar" or "bestower of blessings," and is a commonly used title in India to refer to someone who is God-realized. In his case, it is not a title, but his legal name, as entered in the government records when certain spiritual phenomena first started happening around him. Previously known as Kalki, he had dropped that name because it refers to the tenth incarnation of Vishnu, one who was promised in the Hindu scriptures to come at the end of the Kali Age to promote righteousness and heal the world. The significance of that name had created too much controversy.

In this context, Bhagavan acknowledges that if this is true for himself, it is also true for all others who feel that their mission is to bring healing and enlightenment to the planet. Just as for many Christians, the Second Coming of Christ refers not to a single person but to a collective force of unified consciousness, so is Kalki a collective avataric presence. Anyone who is enlightened, and is working for the enlightenment of humanity, is an aspect of Kalki!

I also want to emphasize again here, especially for Western readers, that the Bhagavan I speak about in this book is not the well-known spiritual teacher Osho, also referred to as Bhagavan.

Bhagavan is an avatar, which can be defined as a descent of divine consciousness into humanity. Within the Hindu tradition, an avatar manifests during a time when our spiritual development has stagnated, and when we need a form of divine intervention in order to move us forward.

There are many kinds of avatars, and each avatar's role is specific. Avatars can work on many levels of consciousness, which can be classified as either earthly or cosmic in nature. For example, Einstein was an avatar of physics, Gandhi was an avatar of nonviolence, Jesus was an avatar of love, and Ramana Maharshi was an avatar of wisdom. Bhagavan's own special mission, along with that of his wife, Amma, is to be an avatar of enlightenment, a "*mukti* avatar." They are often considered to be a single avataric consciousness in two bodies.

Meeting him was an unforgettable experience. We experienced Bhagavan as a warm, wise, pragmatic, and very transparent human being. When asked about what he did, he said that he transmitted states of enlightenment through a process known as the *deeksha*.

Enlightenment cannot be earned, he stated. If this were true, all the millions of spiritual seekers in every age should have been enlightened by now. It could, however, be given. He referred to himself as a technician, and said that it was possible to permanently enlighten the consciousness of the seeker by shifting the neurobiological structure of the brain. What an astounding claim!

I watched my reactions to this statement. Having lived many years in the West, and always wary of being duped by yet another guru with something to sell, a red flag immediately went up in my mind. *Isn't enlightenment something you have to earn for yourself?* I wondered. *How can someone give it to you?*

Still, we both felt a strong resonance with his words, and an excitement in our hearts. We happened to be at Amma's birthday darshan in Nemam when the first public deekshas were given, and immediately afterward enrolled in a weeklong mukti program and received a couple more deekshas. I watched Grace go through a process of transformation, resulting, a few days later, in her enlightenment.

We had both been on a spiritual path for a long time, and had steadfastly practiced all kinds of meditation practices, psychotherapies, healing techniques, and metaphysical teachings, but neither of us had ever experienced anything close to what was happening here. We knew in our hearts that this was the reason we had been led to India.

We talked with Bhagavan after Grace's enlightenment, and I asked him why it was that I hadn't become enlightened, as Grace had. He told me that he could give it to me immediately if I so chose, but that I could be of greater service to humanity if my process were somewhat slower. If it happened quickly, I would not be able to observe it as keenly. Part of my soul's purpose, he said, was to teach this and to write about this.

I was relieved, and excited by this new revelation. I had wondered if there was something wrong with me, whether I hadn't prepared enough, or whether I wasn't worthy: all the countless explanations offered up by the mind when something it thinks it wants does not happen. He assured me that there was nothing I needed to do or not do, and that it would happen soon. In that moment, I realized that my search had already ended. My entire life had been driven by the need to help humanity move into the Golden Age; now, the next level of my work could begin. "You have a destiny," Bhagavan told me, "and it will be fulfilled."

I believe that Bhagavan could well be a key vehicle for the inauguration of the Golden Age. As he emphasizes, however, the name Kalki does not refer to himself alone, but to the collective avataric consciousness that humanity is emerging into. As each of us becomes enlightened, we too enter into this Kalki consciousness. This book is the story of a particular avatar who has learned to give enlightenment to people through a neurobiological process. Yet it is also the story of an unprecedented descent of avataric presence, here to awaken all of humanity as we approach the birthing of a new age.

Bhagavan claims that humanity is on the threshold of a mass enlightenment, perhaps similar to what Sri Aurobindo and the Mother envisioned as the descent of the supramental force. He says that once a critical mass of people become enlightened, then mass enlightenment will begin. Bhagavan's mission is to prepare this critical mass so they can enlighten the rest of the world. Once this happens, it will effortlessly solve the environmental, political, social, and economic crises that loom before us today.

"Enlightenment is very easy," ended Bhagavan as Grace and I got up to go, "and everyone should get enlightened." My hope is that this book will inspire many to do so. After all, Bhagavan says, it is only the beginning of the true spiritual riches that are available to us as incarnated souls.

In the days that followed, I witnessed extraordinary miracles taking place around me every day, performed not only by Bhagavan, but also by countless enlightened people, ranging from physical healings to divine assistance to rainmaking to raising the dead. But the most amazing miracle of all was to watch someone going through the enlightenment process.

My research into the evolutionary history of humanity had convinced me that a shift was imminent, and that a new species of humanity was being birthed. Here, I was seeing history unfold before my own eyes! Thousands have received enlightenment since this phase of the work began in August 2003, and the pace continues to increase exponentially.

What does this mean for each of us personally? If you have read this far, you are probably beginning to feel the echoes within your own soul calling for this divine gift. How do you begin this journey of freedom? How do you break free from the control and limitations inherent within the human condition? You may wish to mull over the following statements, seeing if they resonate with you, before proceeding further:

- The human self, or ego, is programmed for separation, which is the cause of human suffering.

- Enlightenment is the shift from ego to essence.

- Enlightenment is a neurobiological event, which can happen through grace. All the spiritual practices in the world are only a preparation for this possibility.

- The planet is in danger of extinction. Only a planetary enlightenment will save humanity.

- Grace has descended. Enlightenment is now available for the masses.

- Thousands have become enlightened already, without preparation or struggle.

- The world needs to know this now. There is no longer time for anything else.

3.

The Process Begins

In February 2004, six months after Grace's enlightenment, we returned to Oneness University to teach at another Experience Festival. We decided to stay on for a while afterward, so I could gather material to write this book. We observed countless numbers of people receiving the deeksha, and going through an enlightenment process. It was truly amazing.

Yet I still hadn't gone through my own enlightenment. When I first started writing this book, I felt that I should write the bulk of it from the unenlightened state in order to relate better to where I thought people might be, and then add a chapter at the end about my own experience of it. (I was also a little concerned that I might go into a nonfunctional state of deep *samadhi* for some time afterward, and not be able to think well enough to write.)

When I showed the early manuscript to one of the direct disciples of Bhagavan, and shared my reasoning with her, she pointed out that in order to truly relate to the human condition, I would need to go through my own enlightenment first. Until then, I could relate only to myself, and my own ideas of what the world needed. She noticed that I had used a lot of metaphysics, and further added that Bhagavan's teachings are not metaphysical at all: They are purely empirical. In response to my fears about not being able to write, she laughed. Without the interference of the mind's constant chatter, she said, I would be able to focus as never before.

I recognized that underneath my questions was an issue of trust. I had grown to rely on my mind to perform in a certain way, and was afraid that I would not have access to the same clarity and flow that I thought was "mine." My mind delivered a vision of losing my self and becoming a mindless, blithering idiot. As I shared this with her, she laughed again, and affirmed that not only would I have access to all the positive inspiration I was already familiar with, but that the entire universe would be able to write through me!

I realized that I was seeing the universe as somehow separate from myself, somehow less capable of understanding and living out my destiny than I was capable of doing through my own efforts. Even though I lived much of my life from the sense of a divine indwelling presence, it wasn't with total, unconditional trust. I didn't fully believe that the universe was a conscious, living intelligence. A part of my mind still held onto the idea that if "I" disappeared, then the universe would somehow muck it up for me. I had not experienced the universe as a divinely conscious, supremely intelligent, constantly evolving, synchronistic force of wisdom and beauty. I knew that it was true, but did not experience it fully. After all my years of exploring metaphysical truths, it was still very much a concept to me.

I saw that in sharing my ideas of what was happening at Oneness University, I had relied heavily on teachings and concepts. Much as I resonated with the teachings, I had not had the direct experience, and so could only talk about them from an indirect, metaphysical perspective. It was wonderful metaphysics, but it wasn't direct empirical experience. I realized that I would have to rewrite much of what I had written, and that only if I wrote from direct experience would my words have impact.

I also realized that I had a concept of God that was still subconsciously associated with punishment or indifference. I didn't quite trust that God could be my best friend and partner, and was actively interested in my highest happiness. I still believed in a God who was constantly out to test me, to put hurdles in my path so that I could prove my worthiness and love. I still believed that I should continue to suffer for my highest good. It was this version of God that prevented me from actively surrendering to my own enlightenment. It is up to each of us to design the version of God we choose to interact with, says Bhagavan, but he invites us to remember that a jealous or punishing version of God is much less likely to give us this profound gift of grace.

Within minutes of these realizations, another direct disciple of Bhagavan came to tell me that they were going to put me through the enlightenment process starting the following day. Unlike the normal five-day courses, this would be a longer course for teachers. It would include the empowerment to transfer deeksha to other people.

There were six other people in my process group. It lasted seventeen days, and has truly been the most magical experience of my life.

I understand now that because I had spent my whole life studying and practicing metaphysical teachings, my mind was full of concepts about God, concepts about soul, concepts about the universe, concepts about love, and concepts about what enlightenment should look like. All these got obliterated. For much of my life, I had been forcing my experiences to fit into preexisting concepts. With the concepts gone, I could now directly experience truth!

Afterward, the book began to rewrite itself. I decided to start with my own experiences, instead of leaving them for the end. I realized that the teachings would be effective only if accompanied by personal experience. When they substitute for the experience, teachings are worse than useless: They take us even deeper into the traps of the mind. It is only while glimpsing the experience that the teachings can be truly assimilated.

I received seven deekshas during the course of the enlightenment process, spread out over seventeen days. A deeksha is a hands-on transfer of power, channeled by the member-guides of Oneness University. When the deeksha is given, it sets into motion a series of neurobiological shifts within the brain. Certain areas in the frontal lobes of the brain get activated, while other areas within the parietal lobes get deactivated, eventually resulting in a totally different perception of reality, known as the enlightened state. Additionally, the corpus callosum, which connects the two brain hemispheres, is energized, allowing the brain to synchronize and work together, further stimulating the 90 percent of the brain's functions that lie dormant in most of us.

As I received each deeksha, it created changes in my neurobiological structure, resulting in altered states of consciousness, accompanied by powerful insights. The peak experience following a deeksha usually lasts for six to twelve hours, sometimes more. During the course of one of these deekshas, I realized that what I had to do was not to write the book, but to *become* the book. My own process and experiences during the deekshas would serve as the blueprint for anyone reading about them in such a way that the teachings could take hold, and the deeksha itself could be transferred through the sharing. But for this, I would have to be transparently honest.

There is only One Mind. Even though the details of our lives are different, the content of each mind is basically the same: jealousies, longings, insecurities, passions—and on and on and on. The sharing of my own process could thus stimulate an identical process within each person, and act as a deeksha.

This is my intention for the next few chapters. Each chapter includes Bhagavan's teachings, as shared by my guide, followed by the corresponding experience in the deeksha that followed. I have written up many of the teachings as discourses or dialogues. Although they may not be the exact words used, I feel that this will engage the reader in a more immediate way.

Later in the book. I have also included a few chapters entirely devoted to the teachings of enlightenment; by then, you will have a wider context to put those teachings into! You may even begin with those chapters if you wish, or go back and forth for clarification.

I have felt Bhagavan's presence guiding the entire process, from the timing of the process, to orchestrating my deeksha experiences, to inspiring the creative energy that flows through these writings. Regarding my earlier fear that I would be reduced to mindlessness after enlightenment, all I can say is that my mind has never been sharper or more focused, never more receptive to fresh new ways of expression, never more present in each and every moment.

On your part as the reader, please begin this journey with the intention of deeply experiencing your own responses. You may wish to make a link with Amma and Bhagavan through their pictures in the back of the book, and invite their grace as you begin your own process. This does not need to conflict with your religious beliefs. Once you experience enlightenment, you realize that all the faces of God are part of the same oneness, which also includes your own face. Or you may simply call upon your own concept of Divinity to guide your journey.

There is a mantra used at Oneness University that may also prove beneficial. It is known as the Moolamantra. Invoking the divine consciousness of the Supreme One in all its unmanifest and manifest forms, it is as follows:

OM Satchidananda Parabrahma
Purushottama Paramatma
Shri Bhagavati Sameta
Shri Bhagavate Namaha

Friend

Ah, my friend
I see you shrouded in the mist
Reaching out your hand of light
Beckoning me to follow.
How long have you been waiting?
How long have I been afraid?
Who is the self that is afraid to die?
Soon I must run now,
Like a moth to the flame,
Like a river to the sea.
The past is real no more.
What is there to fear
When fear itself melts away
In the fires of living presence?
I look into the mist
Unveiled at last, my Friend stands before me
In blazing, undying light,
Holding out his arms,
Wearing my own face—
There is only one of us here!

4.

Sewers of the Mind

"The mind is like a sewer," said our teacher and guide, as he began to share Bhagavan's teachings with us. "We cover it up with a golden lid, but the stink comes through anyway. It fills the entire house, but we are so busy admiring the golden lid that we don't perceive it. We do not know who we are. The lid is composed of other people's concepts of ourselves, which is the only way we know to refer to ourselves. We get attached to these images of ourselves.

"Instead of cleaning out the sewer," he continued, "we keep staring at the golden lid, which only takes us away from what we know ourselves to be, all the miserable, self-serving, loveless insecurities, comparisons, judgments, lusts, and pains that we try so desperately to cover up. Someone tells us how helpful we've been, so we try to go around helping everybody, however empty we feel, just so we can feel good about ourselves. We believe that we are nasty, so we project that out into the world around us, so people will treat us the way that we believe we deserve to be treated. We are always reinforcing our concepts about ourselves.

"These concepts are like a dead rat in the middle of the room. We sweep it under the rug, but the stink is there. So we cover it up with a bigger rug, or spray perfume into the air, but eventually the stink will come back even stronger. We need to find the rat and remove it.

"The biggest stink comes from our concepts of spirituality and enlightenment. We substitute the concepts of enlightenment for the experience of enlightenment. We think enlightenment is saintliness, so we try to move toward saintliness. We think enlightenment is knowledge, so we try to move toward knowledge. We think enlightenment is perfection, so we try to move toward perfection. We lock ourselves up in the prison of our own mind—all our concepts, expectations, and ideals.

"When the deeksha is given, it has to break its way past all your self-concepts. If you can begin emptying out these concepts, and honestly witness the truth about yourself in your unenlightened state, that will help. Start looking at your masks and cover-ups, all your manufactured emotions, all your self-reproach, and all your insecurities. It is only when you authentically see yourself for what you are that the grace can come.

"When we see ourselves in our vulnerabilities, when we allow our deepest fears to surface, we are no longer dangerous to ourselves or to others. Paradoxically, it is only when we accept our ugliness that we can be truly free. We become like a little child. We no longer need the golden lid to cover up the stink, and can go clean up the sewers instead. This is what the first couple of deekshas will do," added our guide. "They will help you open up the sewers.

"Cleaning them out is simply a matter of honest observation. It is like peeling an onion. The onion is being peeled, but even when you get to the bottom, the peelings are still there. Enlightenment doesn't mean the onion disappears: it means there is no concept of an onion left to hide behind. We see our fears, but they do not rule us. We see our lusts, but don't cover up. We see our insecurities, but accept them.

"We do not have to get to the bottoms of our sewers," continued our guide. "That is the trauma of perfection. If we see only one of our neurotic dramas all the way through, it will be enough. The grace will come. Do not create another expectation about how or when it should happen.

He looked at me directly. "There is a difference between metaphysical knowledge and empirical experience," he said. "We metaphysically create the ideal of a soul, and create immense conflict in our minds the more we try to live up to this ideal image. The more specific our image of perfection, the further away we find ourselves from it, the more elaborate the masks we have to put on, and the more conflict and pain we suffer. The longer we are on a spiritual path, the more concepts we have built up, and the harder it is to let go.

"Empirical knowledge is about being true to yourself in your experience of the moment. The more honest you are with yourself, the more you will see how the unenlightened person is built up of masks, expectations, and ideals, all of it to cover up insecurities, self-reproach, loneliness, and loss of soul. Start with that; explore that. The deeper you go into this core of ugliness, the less you will feel the need to fear it, and the more you will come out of your conflict and suffering."

The mind is such a little thing in the vastness of experience, I realized. We hold onto our little thoughts when the whole universe is rushing by. We let metaphysical concepts choke us when truth is so very simple. An enlightened person who looks at a tree is simply looking at a tree. The unenlightened person builds up concepts about it, such as *Ah! I am in cosmic communion: I have become one with the tree!* There is nothing to become. Enlightenment is to see reality as it already is.

"Sometimes we go about pitying ourselves," goes an ancient Ojibway saying, "and all the time we are being carried on great big winds across the sky."

———

The first deeksha was to be given that evening. Our guide warned us again that the purpose of this deeksha was to make us examine the sewers of our minds. Until an alcoholic "hits bottom," he or she cannot overcome slavery to alcohol. Likewise, unless we fully experience the slavery of our minds, why should we seek liberation?

As we sat in the teaching hut, two more guides came in. As they began to open up to Bhagavan's energy, they went into high states of divine ecstasy, and their bodies became channels for Bhagavan's grace. As we went forward, one by one, these deeksha guides placed their hands upon our heads, and initiated the process of neurological restructuring.

After the deeksha was given, we were asked to go into our rooms and lie down. Gradually, a great sense of uneasiness began to grow within me. My social persona began to dissolve, and I began to see in great detail the games I played with people in order to manipulate them and get my own way, all the while attempting to present an image of myself as kind, loving, wise, honest, and spiritual. I saw how I judged and compared, and how I was jealous and resentful, all the while desperately trying to convince myself that I was spiritually evolved.

I watched my aggression and rage; then, I watched the suppression of my aggression and rage. I watched the conflicts within my mind as I struggled to forgive, still resentful on the outside, still plagued by guilt on the inside. I watched my need to be perfect, my need to be special, and my need to be unique. I watched myself reacting defensively to any assault, real or imaginary, against the cherished spiritual identity that I had so carefully built up throughout the years.

I witnessed with horror the ugliness of my mind, which Bhagavan defines as any kind of self-centered activity. I could see this extending into even the most spiritual of motivations. Was I being good because I was conditioned to be good? Was

I striving to impress someone with my saintliness? Was I helping because I was afraid to say no? Did I love because I wanted to be loved back? Did I want to be recognized for being wise or wonderful? Did I feel so empty inside that I ran from workshop to workshop, filling myself up with every high that came my way? Did I talk about "dying to myself," only to use it as yet another building block in my spiritual edifice? Did I want to be in total charge of my life, even when I stated that I was in service to the Divine? Did I feel the need to achieve enlightenment by my own efforts, so that I could finally, proudly place the crown of enlightenment upon my own head?

I saw how needy and inauthentic my entire life had been. I saw that this wonderful personality that I had thought myself to be was nothing but a mind-controlled robot. As I continued to observe, I noticed that throughout the years I had built a whole set of identities around myself. The spiritual identity was the worst one of all. I was a spiritual teacher and a healer. I was sensitive and compassionate. I was a good person. I had a mission to heal the world. I was wise and loving and deep. I saw that I had become so identified with this image of myself that these very identities had become a mask. I saw how I had carefully protected this image, lest someone see through me into a place that was vulnerable or uncertain, angry or lustful, unloving or fearful, ordinary or shallow, depressed or shy.

I saw my desperate attempts to gain approval, acceptance, and love. I noticed how I was eating up the world around me in order to survive. More is beautiful; bigger is better. I noticed how true this was for me, whether this had to do with a material identity or with spiritual experiences. I noticed how I was dressing up my vices to become virtues. My fear of others became my "need for solitude." I cultivated "humility" because I didn't have the courage to stand up to abuse. I "loved" because

I was afraid to be alone. I had a mission to "save the world" because I didn't have any other planet to go to. I couldn't find any love anywhere. I recognized how unloving I really was, how fragile and hollow my ego was.

I realized that I didn't really like people. I related to them for what they could give me, whether it was love, things, money, recognition, or opportunities for advancing myself. Perhaps they would recognize my light or tell me some nice things about myself. Or perhaps it would give me a chance to tell myself that I was better, wiser, more advanced, more learned, or more loving than they were. Or perhaps I got to feel touched and warmed by their light, because I didn't really believe in my own.

I didn't much like myself either. I saw that I was forever comparing myself with others, and that my sense of self came from how I felt others perceived me, and whether I thought I was good enough or lovable enough or beautiful enough. And so I had to put on my best face at all times. I had lost my sense of spontaneity and wonder. I had lost my ability to live from my soul. Indeed, I doubted if I had ever really known my soul. All I knew was a spiritual labyrinth of the mind.

Then, my mind began to play insidious tricks on me. Afraid of giving up its hold, the mind began to generate uglier and uglier versions of itself. I found myself experiencing enormous depression, self-condemnation, paranoia, and pain, desperately feeding this last illusion as if it were the only thing that was real. I found myself reliving the conditioning of original sin from my teenage years. I was an unworthy being crawling in the dust, meriting only suffering. Indeed, it was this suffering alone that redeemed me, and the more I suffered, the more I was redeemed. Suffering, it seemed, was the ultimate meaning of my life.

I went further back, to the conditioning of my early child-hood. My needs didn't matter. Only others mattered. I didn't exist for myself. I was nothing. I was powerless. I felt empty. I suddenly realized that my lifelong struggle for enlightenment had its origins in this longing to give meaning to this emptiness.

That was it. I had reached the bottom of the sewage tank. There was nothing more that the mind could churn up. I drifted off to sleep.

Strangely, during the course of this deeksha, I had felt an enormous wave of relief each time a realization hit me. It was a relief to crawl out of my hole of self-pity and self-condemnation, it was a relief to take off the masks of spiritual ego, and it was a relief to see the ugliness of my mind, so that I could give up the struggle. I saw that the struggle was only the "me" trying to convince itself that I was good, as opposed to something else that was "not me," which I could identify as bad. I was continually projecting this badness onto other people or outer circumstances or shadow (subconscious) aspects of myself.

When I could see myself in all my ugliness, I could finally come to terms with reality. I wasn't frightened by it anymore. I no longer needed to resist it, or even to take it personally. I even became a bit bored with the whole drama. After all, it wasn't even my own mind. "Strangely," our guide had said, "when you see your ugliness clearly, you no longer need to act it out. When you see your ugliness clearly, you no longer need to behave in an ugly way." When I gave up trying to look good, I could truly be myself. My war with the universe was over!

5.

Multiple Personalities

"There are always two sides of the mind," began our guide one morning, "the good and the bad, the right and the wrong, the ideal and the real. They are always in conflict with each other.

"The unenlightened person, chooses the brighter of these sides and identify with it, calling this 'himself.' Everything else then becomes the contents of the self. They become 'his' thoughts; they become 'his' emotions. Enlightenment is recognizing that there is no such self, that the two sides of the mind are equally my personalities.

"We are always looking at reality from a relative perspective," he continued. "A river is only defined by its banks. Our minds contain our thoughts like a pot contains pebbles. We need a relative object to define ourselves, relative thoughts to define our self. Enlightenment is breaking this container.

"We jump from one side of our mind to the other; we have hateful thoughts and then tell ourselves we shouldn't have such hateful thoughts, that we should forgive, or that they didn't mean it, or couldn't help themselves, or that they deserved it, whatever justifications or rationalizations we use to excuse our own hatefulness.

"The hatefulness is disowned, we pretend it's not 'ours.' We create an idealized image of ourselves, and call it our 'self.' As we study metaphysics we even call this our 'soul,' and the soul becomes all good, as opposed to our thoughts and feelings, which need to be purified, and so we embark on our work of purifying our dark side, or the 'subconscious,' to make it more acceptable."

I noticed my resistance to this concept. The mind doesn't like to have its illusions smashed. I didn't like to think of not having a soul, which was, by definition, divine and permanent. To me, absence of permanence meant nonexistence, and this ran counter to my most cherished beliefs about the nature of the soul and the universe. Our guide pointed out that all I had was metaphysical concepts, and that I was trying to fit an experience into these concepts. It isn't that the soul doesn't exist, he said, but before enlightenment, it's only a concept. After enlightenment, I would have an entirely new experience of it. In fact, my experience of myself would be the soul experiencing itself.

As I pondered his words about the split in consciousness created by our minds, I realized that we even project this split onto our concepts of God. In most of the world's religions, God is good, wise, loving, powerful, and so on. Because we cannot conceive this God as also mirroring the negative personalities, we create the devil, or the equivalent, who is conveniently and proportionately evil.

And what does it reveal about our collective human psyche that God is usually perceived as an authoritarian male figure? Bhagavan emphasizes that God is both male and female, depending on which aspect of God you are relating to.

"We cannot escape the negative personalities," emphasized our guide. "They are parts of ourselves. Our continuous efforts to maintain the sense of ideal selves means that we are also continuously denying, suppressing, condemning, or projecting these negative personalities onto others and ourselves." In a flash of insight, I realized that much of my spiritual search had been about trying to escape my negative personalities. I also realized with painful clarity that many of my concepts of the soul were nothing but my mind's attempts to further elevate the self. It is the mind's way of trying to create its own enlightenment.

"The unenlightened person may develop a seeker personality that seeks to become enlightened," continued our guide. "Yet the seeker is also part of the river and doesn't know it!

"There is no person, only personalities. There is no thinker, only thoughts. After enlightenment, this is perceived very clearly. There are only bubbles of consciousness coming up and passing away, coming up and passing away in the great silence. During the peak experience of enlightenment, even these bubbles cease, and all that is left is the emptiness, the great silence, bliss. After the peak experience is over, my relationship with my mind is forever changed. There is no ownership of my thoughts, and therefore no duality. The good, the bad, and the ugly all have equal residence—and no residence. None of them are understood to be real anymore, none of them are fixated as the self, and therefore none are given preference over any other.

"The unenlightened person labors under the illusion that there is a continuity of self," said our guide. "There are some who believe in the reality of a self, others who believe that there is no self. Bhagavan says that self as a fixed, permanent entity is an illusion. What exists is consciousness arising and falling in every moment and through every experience. When the deeksha is given, the brain is restructured in such a way that it becomes capable of observing the endless stream of personalities, each with its own mental content, each rising up and then falling away. It is like taking a 35-millimeter movie and slowing it down, so you can begin to observe the separate frames of existence.

"When you are enlightened," he continued, "there is no more necessity to judge or compare. You witness the entire dance of creation taking place inside you, but without identifying with any of it. You recognize that each of your personalities, each seeming center of identity, is equally transient. You are not attached to the positive personalities, nor do you condemn the negative personalities. It is like bubbles of transient existence coming up, moment by moment, and then dissolving. Thoughts, feelings, and sensations rise up, and then fall away into the silence. You are no longer able to find a single, continuous self that you define as 'you.'"

Our guide used the example of smashing a mirror. "Which one of these pieces is you?" he asked. "Or think of a spray bottle," he said. "Which of these droplets of mist is you? Is there such a thing as a river separate from the water that flows through it, or a wall separate from the bricks? How, then, could there be a self, separate from these personalities that come and go?"

I recalled the years when I worked as a psychotherapist at Pocket Ranch Institute. Many of our clients had been diagnosed with what was then called multiple personality disorder (MPD). Whenever a different personality would come up, an entirely different set of personality traits would emerge. One personality could be a three-year-old traumatized girl, another could be a teenage male protector, and another could be a thirty-five-year-old professional artist.

Whichever personality was up, it was as if that personality "owned" the body. Each personality was surprised and offended to realize that others were sharing the body, and especially to think that there might be a host personality that included all of them.

It was like a revolving door of personalities. Each personality had different memories, different emotions, and different perceptions of age, gender, self, and the world. Each had a different sense of the body, which even influenced measurable physiology. One personality would have diabetes or multiple sclerosis, another would be perfectly healthy. One would have 20/20 vision, another would be blind. One would be a public speaker, another would be mute. In one instance I heard about, even the blood type changed! The body molded itself to the individual perceptions of every personality. MPD is perceived as a disorder. But in the light of Bhagavan's teaching that we are a series of personalities, rather than a single, fixed self, could MPD actually be an important mirror for humanity, a tool for our evolutionary advancement, given so that we may grow to understand our own true nature?

"Examine all the different personalities," our guide was saying. "During the course of a day, these might continually change, even moment to moment. There is no such thing as a permanent personality, just as there is no such thing as a permanent self."

I started looking at my own multiplicity. A curious and generally receptive personality shows up in class, followed by one who just wants to lie in the sun and do nothing. I feel scolded, and so a very young, shy, and insecure personality comes up, and, sometime later, a wild, aggressive one. Now, the writer shows up, who can't wait to put this information down in words, accompanied by the spiritual teacher. The metaphysician shows up, feeling a bit put off because his spiritual concepts have just been challenged, followed by the doubter.

Soon the seeker shows up again, driving my search for enlightenment, followed by one who is resentful for having wasted so much of his life on an empty search. Then come the commentator and the editor, taking turns to stand apart and watch the rest of the personalities revolving in and out. I want something that I cannot seem to get, and the manipulator comes up. I don't get what I want, and the victim shows up. The loser, the lover, the critic, the peacemaker, the fearful one, the terrorist, the martyr, the tyrant . . . the list goes on and on.

What is the potential for healing once we understand that all our symptoms are simply generated and contained within certain personalities? Equally, what is our potential for manifesting the divine once we become totally devoid of the sense of a separate self?

"Upon enlightenment," continued our guide, picking up my thoughts, "even the sense of the body as a separate entity disappears, and is seen as simply another personality as well. When you become enlightened, you become very fluid. You are not separate from a tree, a dog, or a bird. Your boundaries dissolve. You become the body of the universe, for the universe to dance through!"

———

That evening we received our second deeksha. As the power of the deeksha intensified, the dance of personalities became very clear. I saw that for every positive personality, there was a negative one; and that for every negative personality, there was a positive one. There were hundreds of these personalities. Some were deep-seated, long-term personalities; others came and went, only for that moment. A personality could be created from every experience in life. Now, I was even creating a personality whose only job was to discover new personalities! I made a long list of these in my mind, became overwhelmed, and then finally gave up.

I had come to terms with the self-centeredness of my mind during the first deeksha, so I did not feel much of a charge as I watched the negative personalities come up. The more I allowed them to be, the friendlier they seemed to become. The more I was able to perceive my mental-emotional states as distinct personalities, the less I felt attached to any one of them, and the more empty I felt of a sense of self.

I realized that when I was empty of self, the personalities could come and go fluidly. When "I" resisted or tried to change a personality, such as hurt, doubt, or anger, either by condemning it or suppressing it, the emotional charge would build up, and I would start feeling uncomfortable in my solar plexus. If I noticed this emotional charge and experienced it fully, then it would soon dissipate. As the duality dissolved, which is tantamount to the dissolution of the sense of the separate self, the shadow personalities would flow back together into a unified, stable configuration.

In our work with multiple personalities at Pocket Ranch, we would have the different personalities begin to acknowledge one another's presence, and learn to communicate with one another. I realized that as I acknowledged myself equally as a being of multiple personalities, I was loosening up the fixed self, and, along with it, the entire framework of ifs, buts, and shoulds that had controlled my life.

It was an exhilarating discovery. I continued witnessing the dance of personalities as I dropped off to sleep.

Who Am I?

I look out through your eyes
And see myself looking back—
Who sees who?
A lone cuckoo bird calls out to another
In the early dawn

And I hear my own voice calling back—
Coo who? Coo who?
A gentle breeze
Caresses the tall prairie grass,

A coyote howls at its sister the moon,
The night owl
Swoops towards its own shadow—
Who? Who? Who?
We are all inseparably linked,
Linked from eternity.
You look out through my eyes
And see yourself looking back—
Who sees who?

6.

Mind Struggle

Our guide continued the teachings by discoursing on the nature of mind. "We think that we are separate minds with separate thoughts, but Bhagavan says that, in reality, there is only One Mind. This One Mind has remained unaltered for millennia, ever since the dawn of civilization," he said. "The contents of this Mind may continually rearrange themselves, but the structure has remained the same.

"Bhagavan says that the mind is essentially a computer that functions in certain fixed modes. There are basically four modes of this mind," he went on to say. "The 'defining' mode is continually interpreting reality through preexisting filters. It is not happy until it has analyzed and pigeonholed reality into a form that it can grasp. While looking at a tree, for instance, it is not happy until it can classify the shape, size, color, and botanical name, so that it can then pretend to understand it. When looking at a concept, it is not happy until it has categorized it as true, false, useful, foolish, and so on. When looking at a person, it is not happy until it has determined exactly how useful or useless this person could be to the self.

"Then, there is the 'blaming' mode. Either the mind is turned outward into blaming others, or turned inward into blaming itself; sometimes, it is fluctuating back and forth in confusion." It was not difficult to see how this worked. I blame my partner for making me late, and then feel guilty for not being kind to her. I blame political figures for war on earth, and then blame myself for identical patterns in my daily relationships.

The 'conflict' mode is no better. "There are always two sides of the mind functioning as opposites," he continued. "Should you buy something or not? Is it better to get angry or to hold it in? It requires that you lose touch with the spontaneity of the present moment, and run every decision through the filters of your carefully constructed social persona."

"Finally," he said, "there is the 'becoming' mode. You are never happy being what you are. You cannot stay with the present moment. You are continually looking to a future psychological or spiritual goal or destiny to give meaning to your life. Seeking after enlightenment is the height of the 'becoming' mode of mind.

"Our minds continually run back and forth between these different modes of expression," our guide commented. "It is the journey of our entire lives. We never feel and act spontaneously, and never truly love, because we are constantly separating ourselves from the reality of the moment through these filters of the mind. Not only that, our minds delight in giving us a sense of our own uniqueness, but really, we are all the same. How could we not be? We are all controlled by the same Mind, the same struggles and strategies of survival."

Our guide then read out to us the words of the ancient Indian philosopher Shankara, describing his experience of enlightenment. To paraphrase it, he was saying, "Neither am I wind, nor water, nor earth, nor fire, nor ether. Neither am I the body, nor mind, nor senses, nor soul. Neither am I heaven nor earth nor the worlds in between. Neither am I empty nor full." He goes on for ten stanzas, saying that he is "not this, not that," and then concludes, "All these things I am not. . . . I am pure, blissful Consciousness! I Am That!"

What Shankara is saying is that enlightenment is not something that can be felt or understood or experienced or expressed by the mind or through words, for in pure Consciousness there is no mind and no words, only pure Being. The mind has built-in limitations that cannot be transcended. The closest the mind can get to enlightenment is paradox.

～

The third deeksha was a powerful blast of energy. Silver sandals, representing Bhagavan, were placed on our heads, followed by divine water. After this, three more guides placed their hands upon our heads. Later, as I lay on my bed after the deeksha, my mind went into an intense struggle. Two hours had gone by and "nothing" had happened so far.

I wondered why it was so easy for Grace and for other people, and why it was taking me so long to get enlightened. I alternated between feeling useless, angry, restless, and miserable. I felt listless, as though all energy had been drained out of my body. I wanted to just quit and go to sleep. *Maybe the next deeksha will give me the zap I need,* I thought with resignation.

Our guide came into the room to check in. "How are you?" he asked.

"Nothing is happening," I said.

"Are you so sure?" he inquired. He asked me to describe my state. Then, he asked me what I was expecting enlightenment to look like.

As I talked, I realized that I was expecting enlightenment to be a high, like an LSD trip, an altered state of reality where I would be struck on the head with lightning and immediately go into cosmic consciousness. I was expecting that I would experience what I imagined Shankara had experienced or what Buddha had experienced or what Jesus had experienced.

Our guide made me realize that I was still carrying around a concept about enlightenment, and still expecting that enlightenment should fit into this concept. "Enlightenment is simply about seeing reality as it is," he continued, "not about choosing what reality you want to experience. Whether you are struggling or not makes no difference at all. The process will continue, whether you struggle or not. These are all personalities that come and go. It has nothing to do with Bhagavan's grace. You are still trying to put enlightenment into a box."

I realized that I was still holding the expectation that I could somehow create my own enlightenment, perhaps by finding the most "spiritual" of all my personalities, and bringing it forward. I noticed my fear that somehow I wasn't doing it right, and that therefore I would fail. I noticed that I was caught up in the "becoming" mode of the mind. How foolish I was to assume that I could in any way help or stop the process! My part was to receive the deeksha; the rest was up to God. Understanding this made everything a lot simpler. I relaxed.

Suddenly, my guide stopped me in the middle of a sentence. "Your voice quality has changed," he said softly.

I started feeling an altered state coming on. He asked me to focus on my heart. "Do you feel the silence there?" As I listened, my heartbeat grew louder and louder. "The enlightenment train has left the station. It will be here at seven o'clock," he joked, and left the room.

As I lay in my hut, I began to experience my body dissolving. I put my fingers to my wrist in order to feel my pulse, and suddenly the pulsing expanded to fill my entire body, and then out into space. I couldn't feel the pulse in my physical body anymore. Everything was only this pulse, and I was inside it.

For the next few hours, I was focused entirely on this heart-beat. I felt a tremendous pain in my physical heart from the intensity of a divine presence. It was almost more than I could handle, and I kept breathing into the pain.

Every once in a while, when the energy backed off a bit, I would check to see if I could feel my physical pulse. Every time I tried to, I would once again be taken out into this huge, expanded heartbeat. Sometimes the pain was so strong that I thought my heart would explode; then, it would back off a little, and then come back equally strong. Was this my childhood pain, I wondered? Was this humanity's pain? Was I being shown a glimpse of this so that my heart could open in compassion to the world? It didn't matter. It was all the same. All I could do was stay with the experience, which continued into the early hours of the morning, when I fell asleep.

7.

Letting Go

When I woke up the following morning, there was a deep space within my heart. There was a silence between my thoughts, between my personalities. The silence was so deep that I could drown in it. Was I enlightened? I thought excitedly. I got out of bed, wobbled outside the hut to watch the sunrise, and then came back in and began to journal. After summarizing my experiences of the night before, I continued to ponder:

> When there is no struggle, there is a great silence, not The Great Silence, just a great silence. . . . whenever I capitalize something, it becomes a concept. i need to change the english language and remove all the capitals from it. people would be less self-important if they were simply an i. perhaps that's the cause of our entire mind disease, that we started capitalizing our self.
>
> when you are enlightened, you look at a tree, and you are the tree—simple. there is no self-important "I" relating to the concept of a "Tree" built up over a lifetime of words. no, you look at a tree, there's no you, there's no tree—so you are the tree. you don't even "become" the tree: everything just is the way it is. an unenlightened person looks at the enlightened person looking at the tree, and comes up with all kinds of silly nonsense about Deep Communion and Cosmic Consciousness, but it's only concepts until he experiences it himself.

There were no teachings given the following couple of days. I journaled a lot, catching up on writing about the teachings and experiences of the past few days. I was in a state of crystal clarity of mind: All my thoughts were transparent. I could see how this state of clarity could be quite disturbing for anyone brought up with the concepts of original sin or a punishing God. A couple of people in my group were indeed experiencing paranoid fantasies, as all their self-judgments and assumptions about God came back to them magnified.

I could see that if my concept of God, whether consciously or subconsciously, was of a stern, judging, punishing patriarch, it would make it extremely difficult to trust or surrender to such a God, and to the universe as the playground of God. This concept of God is certainly a hindrance to enlightenment. Within this concept of God, the mind becomes a battleground for personal autonomy, where freedom is found in escaping from this punishing God.

How sad and erroneous this concept is! How much untold suffering, how many wars, have been unleashed in the name of such a God! Upon enlightenment, one realizes that the Divine is simply All There Is, and each of us is a piece of All There Is. In fact, as the ancient Indian *rishis* understood, there is no difference between the individual soul, Atman, and the universal soul, Brahman.

Because it is the same soul, and the same dance, there is never conflict between a personal will and a divine will. They are two aspects of the same reality. We become a joyful expression of the Divine everywhere we go, simply because that is who we are! There is absolute trust and oneness with the universe, which is nothing but benign, nothing but joyful, and nothing but love!

Realizations such as these were moving through me as rapidly as I could write them down. As the time for deeksha neared, I began to fantasize about the next deeksha. I saw myself going into cosmic consciousness and traveling through all kinds of *lokas* (heavenly realms) and meeting all kinds of cosmic beings and discovering all the secrets of the universe.

I fantasized instantaneously transporting myself from place to place, as Babaji did in the Himalayas, giving deekshas to people, watching miracles happening everywhere, just as Christ did, and even more. I watched my spiritual personality having a heyday, while humility and equanimity threw up their hands in despair! Humor came in and told them to move over. "Let the guy have his fantasy in peace!" Which I did, until the next round. . . .

Then, it was time for the fourth deeksha. Like all the ones that were to follow, it was a strong one, with five guides laying on hands in succession!

I lay down in my hut after the deeksha and turned off the fan. It was noisy and I had been experiencing such a deep silence that I wanted to hang onto it, despite the summer heat. That was my first mistake, wanting to hang onto a state. I then started breathing into my heart in order to reconnect with the experience of the one heart from my previous deeksha. That was my second mistake. Why expect to have the same experience twice?

For the longest time, nothing happened. As usual, my personalities of doubt, frustration, self-criticism, and self-pity gathered around. In fact, they came back even stronger, because I had been feeling so good and enlightened before the deeksha.

Then came guilt. Maybe I had just been setting myself up for a fall with all my spiritual fantasizing. Or maybe it was all my training in original sin! I decided to turn the fan back on to drown out the chatter in my head.

Our guide came in. "Were you expecting the big experience?" he asked me right away. I nodded sheepishly. I admitted my fear that I wasn't enlightened, and would never get enlightened. I also admitted my expectation that somehow today's experience needed to be more intense, bigger, and deeper, to prove that I was enlightened.

"How do you know that's what you need?" asked our guide. "Your mind has this concept about enlightenment," he went on. "You are still wanting to arrange your experiences to fit your concepts about enlightenment."

He reminded me that Bhagavan was not interested in the contents of my mind, whatever they were, only that I experience it fully. "It is better that you authentically experience frustration or self-doubt than to have the best high possible and get attached to it!"

I noticed that because of all my expectations and inner conflicts, I was not able to experience what was truly there in the moment. "You are not always where you seem to be," he went on. "It's like a circle. Sometimes the shortest path is the long way around, as long as you keep walking. The mind's struggle with struggle creates an attachment that keeps you stuck there."

He reminded me that the mind does not change upon enlightenment, as most people believe. "No, Bhagavan says that the mind will always be the mind, as ugly or self-centered as ever, but enlightenment means being able to disengage from it. Are you still weighted down with concepts about what this means? Look at what you have been doing: identifying your personalities and dissolving the concept of self. Could you have done this so easily before?"

I argued with him. "Yes, I could do this before. I couldn't always change how I felt, but I could always step back and notice my stuff, even if I wasn't calling it personalities. Are you telling me that this is all that enlightenment is? If that is it, then I was enlightened before I came here!"

As I continued to argue with him, the energy started shifting. I wasn't struggling with struggle anymore. I was caught up in a huge torrent of energy, and dissolved into it.

Later, my guide came back in. "*Enlightenment* is the most karmically loaded word there is." As I looked at him uncomprehendingly, he continued. "All the struggles people have had to seek enlightenment or to get enlightened have become tied up with it. It's like going to the enlightenment web site, www.enlightenment.com, and finding www.struggle.com instead. All the struggle that you are experiencing is part of the field around it."

This was an interesting revelation! "There are so many teachings today, so many different kinds of *sadhanas* and practices, so many paths to get there, but without enlightenment these only manage to generate more craving: craving for enlightenment. The early rishis considered it a sin to talk about enlightenment if they couldn't deliver it. This is why there is such a dense karmic field of frustration and struggle surrounding it."

"Did you have the same struggle with it?" I asked.

"No, Amma showed me this, and then it happened easily!"

"Why is it so easy for some people?"

"Only the very brave or the very foolish think they can take on this struggle and change it," he commented wisely. "The rest just receive it as a gift."

It was at this point that I realized that this was the form my book would have to take, these conversations with my guide. People would much rather relate to somebody's actual experiences, I realized, not just get a bunch of teachings. "Yes, Bhagavan is writing the book," my guide affirmed. "And *you* are the book."

After he left, the magnified heartbeat came back, and with it the pain. It was just as intense as before. I continued breathing into it, allowing myself to feel it fully. For hours, there was nothing but this heartbeat, and the pain. Gradually, toward dawn, it subsided, and I drifted into sleep.

8.

Crossing the Finish Line

The next day, I asked my guide about the pain in my heart. "Don't get excited by the idea that it's the weight of the world." He related an experience where he had once told his inner Bhagavan that all he wanted to do was to help ease the burden that Bhagavan was carrying for humanity. Bhagavan said, "No, please, don't ask for that," but it was too late: He was already feeling the anguish.

After the pain subsided, Bhagavan told him that the best way that he could help was to be joyous, and to help others get enlightened. "People get stuck with an idea of compassion," he said. "If someone were drowning in quicksand, would you want to go and join him in your so-called compassion? Wouldn't you want to find a rope and quickly pull him out? Experiencing true compassion from an enlightened state is very different from conceptualizing about it."

Did I have some kind of an Atlas syndrome, where I wanted to take on the weight of the world in the hopes of transmuting it? Or some kind of martyr complex, where I was willing to sacrifice myself for the world? No matter, it wasn't important. Whatever it was, it had been given to me for a reason, and I accepted that.

We usually had some days off between teachings and deekshas. Even though I was receiving powerful insights and experiences during this time, I could not maintain the states, and my mind would return to its habituated patterns of struggle, questioning, and doubt.

I no longer questioned whether I had gone through enlightenment experiences, but I was still struggling with the question of whether I was permanently enlightened yet. Most of what I remembered experiencing in my most recent two deekshas was pain, and even that was becoming a distant memory. There had been no bliss or cosmic consciousness, no involuntary movements of the body, no hysterical laughter as I suddenly saw the great cosmic joke, no journeys to lokas, and no extraordinary phenomena. I still hadn't seen any visions. "If you're asking the question, you're not enlightened," our guide had said once, so I must not be enlightened. But hadn't he also said that the enlightenment train had left the station?

As I talked with him, I began to see the subtle games my mind was playing. I had been on a spiritual path all my life, doing intense sadhana for twenty years. How could I let go now and risk that I would suddenly get enlightened outside of my own efforts? I still needed to feel in control, even going as far as defining and analyzing my experience of enlightenment!

"It is difficult for spiritual people to let go into enlightenment," said my guide. "It is a paradox. The mind wants to take credit for itself, make all that spiritual work count. What would all the years of meditation be worth if suddenly enlightenment could just be handed to you? Enlightenment is a warrior's path. You work for it as you need to, but when it is all over and done, 'you' can't take credit for it because 'you' are dead."

He related the story of Bhagavan's driver, who had been given the deeksha and immediately got enlightened. His guide asked him what the experience was like. He said, "Before, I was driving the car. Now, the car is driving itself."

I recognized that I was still struggling to hold onto the wheel, trying to understand every step of the journey. Bhagavan was telling me to move over and let him drive, relax and enjoy the ride, or just have an ice-cream cone, and I was saying, *No, I need to see where I am going. I need to control the journey.* I *need to drive* myself *into enlightenment.*

All that I was doing was driving myself up a wall.

—

The fifth deeksha was given. Again, nothing seemed to be happening for a while. This time, however, I knew the territory. I realized that even this perception of "nothing" was a mental concept. Soon, I relaxed into fully experiencing each changing personality, and then felt myself going into an altered state. I began experiencing a deep silence.

I had been working with a practice called the sound current for years, and was familiar with a quality of silence that was profound. But I had never felt any silence this complete. The sound of this silence filled the universe!

My guide came in. "The wave and the ocean are not two," he commented. "Thoughts and silence are not separate. Silence lives below every thought, and pervades everything. It does not matter whether you are speaking or listening, walking down a busy street or meditating."

"It's like one wave watching another wave," I responded. "But it's the same ocean underneath."

"Yes, and self is an illusion that thinks that it is separate from the ocean."

I had always thought of the act of witnessing as somehow stepping outside myself, and watching the rest of me go by. I asked him about this.

"No, that is just another personality," he said. "Witnessing is not a separate thing. It means to not resist the changing nature of the mind, to consciously be with whatever is happening."

"In other words," I responded, "you're talking about 'beingness,' like the tide that continuously comes in and goes back out." I told him that I didn't like the term *witness* in this context, that I preferred to just call it *beingness*.

"Yes," he affirmed. "But you can't even really make a distinction between *beingness* and *oneness*. When you are 'being,' you are one. When there is no self and no other, you are one. It is not a metaphysical oneness, where you somehow 'enter into' or 'become' something or someone, but a recognition that it is the same ocean, the same silence that hangs between you."

I became distracted by an age-old question: Was I the drop or the ocean? Was I the drop merging into the ocean or the ocean merging into the drop? I realized that even this was a meaningless analogy: The drop is an illusion! "Which of these droplets is you?" I recalled the words of our guide.

My mind returned to his words. "When you are totally being with the nature of the mind, seeing how everything just bubbles up and dies away, no sequence, no order, just random thoughts and emotions that come and go, this very 'being' is witnessing. You don't have to forcefully pop out of yourself to see it. You are simply with it, like a cork bobbing in the waves. The concept of self is what tries to keep the cork from bobbing, keep it fixed."

Then, his voice took on a serious tone. "You are at the finish line, Kiara."

"But it's so normal!" I protested.

"Of course. It's still the same mind. You're not changing the mind: You're just not resisting it. Actually, it doesn't even matter if you are resisting or not resisting. Even that can be seen as the flow of the mind. When you're witnessing, you're not fixated in one part of the duality."

"'Being' means that there is no conflict," he continued. "You free up your energy. This energy is bliss."

I could see now what he had meant earlier when he said that any emotion, fully experienced, is bliss. When we can fully accept any of our personalities, conflict ceases. When conflict ceases, all the energy that was locked up in the struggle gets released, and shoots up the *kundalini* channels, causing bliss!

"When you're in doubt, experience the doubt," our guide advised. "When you're in resistance, experience the resistance. 'Beingness' means you simply experience the mind directly, rather than interpreting it through fixed concepts."

I realized that it was not reality itself, but our interpretations of reality that were so oppressive. It is not our suffering, but our attempts to escape from suffering that cause us so much pain!

"Imagine that you're late for an appointment," our guide continued. "The reality is that you're late for the appointment. But then your mind jumps in to interpret it—you're stupid, you can't be trusted, you never show up on time, and so on—and pretty soon, you're not just late, but miserable as well. Plus, all the times in your life that you've been late, and all the times in your life that you've felt the way you feel now, start piling up. It's a wonder more people don't go out and shoot themselves!

"The concept of a self is the dividing line between inner and outer reality," he said after a lengthy silence.

Intrigued, I asked him to say more. "There is really no inner or outer," he pronounced. "That is why a mystical vision can be as real as, or more real than, physical reality. When you lose your self, you become part of the playground of God, whose expression is both physical and mystical.

"Many people consider the physical world to be an illusion. From a metaphysical perspective, this may be true, but from an empirical perspective, it is nonsense. This is where the debate between science and religion often gets bogged down.

'How can you say this table is an illusion,' says the empirical voice of science, 'when all my senses indicate that it is right here in front of me?'

"Rather, it is our perception of the world that is an illusion. It is an illusion because the perceiver is an illusion. The sense of self derives its existence from the configuration of our human neurocircuitry. When the deeksha is given, it alters this neurocircuitry and dissolves this illusory sense of self. This is why Bhagavan says that enlightenment is a neurobiological process.

"When the self disappears, we see reality as it is. When the self disappears, the dividing line between physical reality and mystical reality also disappears. We recognize that it is not the physical world that is an illusion, but the perception that the physical world is separate from the mystical worlds that is the illusion.

"When people become slaves to the idea that the mystical worlds are more profound than the physical world, they naturally distance themselves from truly experiencing the physical reality around them. Even enlightenment is made into a highly mystical experience, when all it means is to be in touch with what is really there."

I realized that this was where I had become stuck. I had equated enlightenment with perpetually living in mystical reality, which arose from my perception that physical reality was somehow inferior to mystical reality. This perception, in turn, removed me from the reality of the present moment, in which mystical and physical realities were one.

"When there is no self, your mind simply becomes another sense," our guide continued. "Watching a thought is like watching a tree. Watching a tree is like watching a vision. They are all equally real, and they are all equally unreal."

This was a revelation. If people could really grasp this, we would be living in a heaven on earth. It would mean completely disconnecting from the consensus reality of the ancient mind, and our relationship with matter itself would be very different. It would mean that all the insights of quantum physics would become true, not just on a micro level, but on the level of our perceptions as well!

While I was pondering the implications of this statement, I suddenly heard him say, "Where is the rule that says every question must have an answer? *Am I enlightened?* you ask. When you realize that doubt itself is nothing to be feared, then that question does not need to be answered.

"You have been dancing around the finish line ever since your third deeksha," he declared authoritatively.

I suddenly realized that I had been expecting enlightenment to get me out of the mind. It wasn't about getting out of the mind, but paradoxically, about fully accepting the nature of the mind. Once I can see it, I am no longer bound by it. Once I can see the mind clearly, it loses its power to fix me in duality. Then, Supreme Intelligence can come through, moment by moment.

I saw clearly that because I had concepts and expectations about enlightenment, I was resisting acknowledging that something powerful had taken place inside my consciousness. It was a subtle shift, but the implications were huge. I had generally been feeling at peace with myself in my life, so the contrast was less than for someone in obvious pain, but I could feel an indescribable quality of peace, silence, and attunement with life that hadn't been there before. It was a peace that arose from the ability to embrace the here and now as a gift from the universe.

I also realized that enlightenment does not have to be a mystical experience of being bowled over by cosmic consciousness. It is simply the realization that the concept of self is an illusion. The self is merely something to fixate on; what is real is a sea of constantly changing personalities. I understood that in losing this fixation, I had made room for the whole universe to dance through me. What felt like a death to the mind was, in actuality, the ability to truly live for the first time, to truly experience reality without the constant interruptions and interpretations of the mind.

I was already familiar with much of this territory. I was in touch with my soul already, and had already experienced a great deal of love, peace, and joy in my life. I already felt a sense of purpose. But I still felt trapped and submerged in the field of duality, however subtle its form. I was still feeling separate from the world, and therefore powerless in my need to change it, or change myself, to fit into my ideal of how it should or shouldn't be.

Now, I knew that I had experienced a shift. I could acknowledge the perfection of all life, even with all the seeming imperfections inherent in the world around me and within me. A great gratitude for Amma and Bhagavan welled up in my heart. I had crossed the finish line.

The Garden

I see a garden beyond the flame
To enter, I must burn away
Everything I have ever identified with,
All the stories I have ever told,
Everyone I have ever known or loved,
All ideas of separation and loss,
Even my yearnings for union.
I must enter empty-handed,
Expecting nothing,

Offering everything I am in return,
Offering my death to the flames.
Such a small price to pay,
So easy now
To enter the garden of life.

9.

Darshan with Amma

The following day, we were invited as a group for a darshan with Bhagavan. As we sat in meditation, my body dissolved into joy, and I felt as giddy as a drunken pigeon for hours afterward. It was all the proof I needed, if I needed more, that something powerful had shifted inside me.

The following day, we traveled to Nemam, where Amma does her *darshans* (spiritual encounters). Although I haven't spoken of Amma very much yet, Amma and Bhagavan are a single avataric consciousness in two bodies. I had asked our guide once why I didn't feel the same connection with Amma as I did with Bhagavan. He said that I probably needed to resolve something in relationship with my own mother. I knew that it was time to change that.

We first attended a public darshan with Amma. There were thousands of people gathered, and their devotion to and connection with Amma was touching. I began to feel the vastness of her being, and went into a state of expanded joy.

Then, we were called for a private darshan with her. There must have been about fifteen of us in the room, and several guides. When Amma came into the room, I felt a wave of love move into me. Amma spoke with each of us and gave us her blessing.

If Bhagavan's mission is about imparting the state of enlightenment, Amma, out of her compassion for people, has chosen to fulfill the desires of their hearts before they seek enlightenment. Unless desires are fulfilled, most people will not have an intense wish for enlightenment. Ordinary human desires are not to be belittled. The divine grace of Amma and Bhagavan comes to the aid of people seeking mundane desires as much as for those seeking enlightenment. We were invited to make requests of Amma.

When my turn came, I dedicated my life to her work of healing and blessing the earth. I asked that her presence be strong within me, and that my wife and I be used powerfully as vehicles for Amma and Bhagavan's grace as we traveled, taught, and gave deeksha. I could see that sharing this blessing was going to become my life. I asked that she use my hands and my feet to bless the world. I also told her about this book that I was planning to write, and asked for her blessing that the book itself would become a deeksha to liberate many.

She smiled, and I felt the enormousness of her being. I felt how an avatar's consciousness pervades the entire cosmos, and that I was a cell within her body, one player within her dream. I understood that the miracles that were reported to be happening on a daily basis in her presence were simply an expression of her immensely giving nature. "I will do it!" she said to me, as she placed her hands on my head to bless me.

I was thrown into a silence that enveloped my physical body and remained in an expanded state of reality for many hours afterwards.

After meeting Amma, I regretted that I hadn't asked her for certain things, such as a more open heart, the gift of healing, mystical vision, and blessings for my family. Our guide told us that Amma read all our wishes and thoughts, spoken and unspoken. Her very nature was to give, give, give. . .

He also told us that divine grace would start manifesting through our bodies as gifts of healing and mukti—whatever was needed in order to most effectively help people. "It is Amma and Bhagavan themselves who are now anchored in your antaryamin (indwelling divinity), and will bring through these gifts."

10.

Cosmic Consciousness

The following day, we had our sixth deeksha. As I went into the deeksha, it was with immense gratitude to Amma. I was so grateful to have met her in Nemam, to balance out the relationship I already had with Bhagavan. I kept repeating, "Amma, Amma, Amma."

While lying in my hut, a few minutes into the process, I heard a taxi pull up, and Grace's voice floated in. She had been gone for the past several days so that I could do my enlightenment process without being distracted, and had returned earlier than I expected. I was just beginning to go into an altered state, and I felt irritated and interrupted. I stumbled out in my deeksha daze and lay on the steps of the hut next door. It was locked, but I knew it was empty.

Soon, a reorganization took place in my consciousness. I realized that there were no accidents, no interruptions, and no separations. All things were in Amma's hands. When my guide came with the keys to the hut to let me in, I was already feeling gratitude for the cosmic order of things. I relayed to him my process. "There is no separation. Everything is sacred and perfect," he affirmed.

I asked Amma to come into my heart, continuing to surrender, continuing to invite her in deeper. Soon, I dissolved into an expanded state. I was no longer Kiara asking Amma to come into his heart, but Amma, inviting Kiara into hers! If she were to come into mine, I could push her out, but where else could I go once I was held within her embrace?

The state continued to deepen. I felt bigger and bigger as my sense of body extended farther and farther out. I didn't have to try to *feel* love anymore: I *was* love.

I found myself giving deeksha to people I knew. My right hand lay on the bed and strong currents would start streaming out as I visualized people. I would feel their suffering in my/her body. After a while, I would feel something transform in them, and eventually the current would trickle down to a halt. As I continued giving deeksha to more and more people, it happened more and more quickly, until eventually, with just a thought, the current would pulse through and go where it was needed.

I then found myself giving deeksha to several people at once. I blessed the world leaders, even those I thought were a menace, and felt the currents flow. *They, too, are part of the divine order,* I realized with joy. There was *no one* outside Amma's grace.

Soon, I was blessing entire countries, the mass consciousness of humanity, and earth itself. When my guide next stopped by, I was in a state of cosmic ecstasy. Everything was my body; and worlds and universes were being birthed in me, dissolving in me. As I breathed out, there was creation. As I breathed in, there was dissolution. I felt vast, vast, vast.

After a while, my guide came back in. "Jagat Mata," I mumbled to him. "You're feeling Jagat Mata?" he asked. "No, I am Jagat Mata, Universal Mother."

After some time, my thoughts turned to Bhagavan. I felt him walking down to the lawn for his evening darshan. I likewise went through the stages of seeing him coming into my heart, entering into my heart, and then dissolving into his cosmic presence. Soon, I was Jagat Pita, Universal Father.

I experienced Bhagavan as the sun, the physical embodiment of solar consciousness; then, I felt him/me expanding farther out yet into the endless galaxies. Again, I created worlds, and I dissolved worlds. As dual aspects of a vast avataric field, I experienced Amma and Bhagavan both containing and expanding each other.

I had been feeling somewhat split about my loyalties between them. Now, I could see that Amma was inside Bhagavan, who was inside Amma, like the yin–yang symbol. They were not separate.

I felt the immense power of Bhagavan. When I was describing it to my guide later, my voice came from deep inside me somewhere as I smashed my fist into my open palm. I could feel the immense energy contained within the body of Bhagavan, waiting to release itself to liberate humanity.

I saw that he could dispel all darkness on earth in one instant. But it is happening gradually, in accordance with cosmic law; gradually enough so that everyone will make it. I knew in that moment that nothing could hold back his *sankalpa,* his divine intention, for world enlightenment. I had wondered how he could know with such absolute conviction—amid all the uncertainties of the day, amid all the environmental, political, and human crises that grow more depressing by the hour—that we wouldn't destroy ourselves as a species.

I could see now that this entire world was an external form of the Divine. It was the Divine's dream, dance, creation. The entire stream of history was a response to a mighty evolutionary impulse. And I knew with absolute certainty that our journey into the Golden Age was assured, and would happen as the Divine's grace intended.

Again, I found myself giving mukti deeksha to people. Unlike Amma's deeksha of grace, however, this was a more selective process. As a few people came to mind, currents of energy would stream out of my hands. When my mind would come up with others, no energy flowed. Two or three people got the full dose, and I will be curious to find out what they experienced. The deeksha had its own divine intelligence.

I realized that there was no Kiara left anywhere. Bhagavan and Amma, as avataric reflections of the Formless One, were everywhere and everything. My body was moving spontaneously, all by itself. I stood and danced the dance of Shiva. At times, the energy would be so intense that I would have to back off from it, take a few breaths, and then reengage.

Often in the past, when I led group meditations, we would go through a process of expansion in our subtle bodies: merging with the group soul and then the soul of the local bioregion and then the national soul and then the planetary soul and then the galactic soul . . . farther and farther out. It would lead to a point where I felt as though the stars would become the cells in my cosmic body. But I had felt that experience only in my subtle bodies. I had never felt this in my physical body, never felt that I could open my eyes and dance, and the universe would dance with me! It was ecstatic beyond words!

"You had asked for cosmic consciousness," said my guide the next time he checked in. "Is this intense enough for you?" I realized that it was about as much as my body could handle.

"That's still not *1 percent* of what they hold in their bodies all the time," he said. "As avatars, their bodies are wired differently."

An avatar's function is to bring new evolutionary potential into the mass consciousness of a species. Is this, I wondered, how our bodies will be wired in future generations? Is this what the "indigo children" are preparing for?

I felt how all the avatars who had ever walked the earth came from this same center of avataric consciousness. There was no separation among them. It was all a single consciousness, and each one of us is now being called into this consciousness.

What I was experiencing was the same consciousness that Bhagavan embodied: not equal to his, but the same. I could now understand what Bhagavan meant about the unity of all things. We are all the same vast avataric presence here on earth to heal and enlighten the planet. Each person who becomes enlightened becomes part of this avataric consciousness, whether we call it Kalki consciousness or Christ consciousness or Buddha consciousness!

I knew also that Amma and Bhagavan's grace, as it is manifesting today, is not even a tiny fraction of what they are capable of giving humanity, and will give humanity in the years to come. But even this tiny fraction is bringing about a huge change. "How much are they capable of holding?" I mumbled stupidly.

"It all depends on what's needed. As much as they need to."

I realize that as we move toward global enlightenment, this will continue to increase. The more people who become enlightened, the stronger the "morphogenetic fields" of enlightenment, through which they can bring even more through—until mass enlightenment takes place!

I saw that this could well be a planetary ascension, a vibrational lifting of all matter on Earth, and not just enlightenment. But that's still ahead: We shall see. I also realized that what Bhagavan and Amma are here to accomplish is much bigger than the earth. I don't have the words or concepts to imagine what this may be, but it feels cosmic in nature.

I found that as I turned my body counterclockwise, the energies would heighten significantly, as though the physical body were becoming an antenna for more of the cosmic energies to anchor down into earth. At one point, as I danced under the stars, I could see that the stars were all part of my body's dance. They were cells in my body, as I am a cell in Bhagavan's body. I was reminded of the story of Indra's net, where the entire universe is made up of pearls, and each pearl is reflected within—and inseparable from—every other pearl.

"This is only the beginning," said my guide. "Your state will continue to deepen even beyond this. It will happen naturally. There is no Kiara now to make it happen or to hold it back now. It is only the Divine working through you."

I began to understand about divine personalities, not just Amma and Bhagavan, but others as well. They could come now and anchor into the earth's frequency fields through this hollow reed that is Kiara's body. I have long felt a connection with Sanat Kumar, one of the cosmic beings who serves as a guardian for the earth. I invited him to come through, and felt a vast consciousness take hold. It was different from Bhagavan's or Amma's consciousness; I can't quite interpret it all yet, but it stayed for a long time, and I felt the Earth embraced within his body.

Then Babaji came through. In 1985, I had become close to him through an enlightenment experience. For months afterward, I had felt his energies coursing through my body almost twenty-four hours a day. Now, I felt him again. He slid right into the physical body, and it seemed to fit him perfectly, as if it were made for him. Perhaps it is, I don't know. I only know that I am a dancing river of joy, not separate from the universe.

Finally, at one point, as I tried to engage my mind to think about how to put a sheet on the musty bed of my new hut, there was a violent reaction in my solar plexus—and I ended up vomiting over the porch wall. I felt an abrupt shift. It was as though I had walked through a thin curtain. No longer was I unified with cosmic consciousness. I was still held within the vast embrace of Amma and Bhagavan, but the experience of conscious unity was beginning to disappear.

I understood suddenly what Jesus had meant when he said, "I and the Father are one." It is the experience of cosmic consciousness. When he says, "I am the way, the truth and the life," it is not the personal Jesus who is speaking: It is the cosmic consciousness speaking through his body.

The following morning, thoughts were back, but not in the old way. And Kiara was back, but not in the old way either. I wrote in my journal, "Before, I was one. Now, I am not-one. But I am not two either. I can understand Shankara's experience now. My hand moves as my mind moves me. Consciousness itself moves me, not some fixated little self who was illusory to begin with. My body is an empty shell for the whole universe to use. Meanwhile, the biological consciousness permeates it and empowers it. The body is such a sacred thing. It is a temple for the Holy Spirit. I understand this for the first time now. I must take care of it.

"Empty, yes, but oh so full—not stuffed with the measly concerns of a petty nonexistent self anymore—but as full as the entire universe!

"There is no person now. Kiara is empty."

II.

Empowerment

The day after this experience of cosmic consciousness was a strange one for me. After experiencing the perfection and order of the cosmos, it was difficult to come to terms with the imperfection and mundane quality of everyday life. Why was everybody talking about such inconsequential stuff? Why did people have to whine about everything all the time?

I realized that there is always balance in the universe. After the experience of expansion, my consciousness was now going into a contraction, and all the old pathways of judgment and comparison held in my body were being stimulated. Once I could see it for what it was, the feeling gradually dissipated. I realized that there is an order and perfection, even in all the seeming contradictions and imperfections.

I spoke with our guide about it. "There is perfection in the world of duality, too, but only after you accept the ugliness of the mind, and no longer have a need to be living out an ideal. That is why Bhagavan says these two foundation stones are so important: ugliness of mind and the impossibility of changing the mind. If this foundation is strong, you can go as high as you please, and you won't come crashing down. Once you get it, you no longer need to suffer emotional downswings, because depression only comes when you expect that you can change the mind and make it better. We simply see reality as it is, and are not attached to any one version of ourselves, which we have to feed, protect, and defend.

"An enlightened person doesn't have to be a saint. The Buddha lost his temper on several occasions. Nor are all saints enlightened, for that matter. It's two totally separate things."

He went on to talk about the difference between enlightenment and God-realization. "God-realization means simply to have a direct experiential connection with God. An enlightened person is not always God-realized. Nor is a God-realized person necessarily enlightened. The Buddha was enlightened, but he wasn't God-realized. All craving stopped, even the craving for God, when he discovered the absence of self. He experienced the emptiness of self, but did not go on to experience the fullness of God. Many Sufis and poet-saints of India, on the other hand, were God-realized, but they were not enlightened. They were so intent on loving God that they couldn't wish for anything more."

"Wouldn't union with God be an equally, if not more, profound realization?" I asked.

"Perhaps, but they weren't interested in that. They feared that enlightenment would dissolve the self, which would put an end to their dualistic attitude of service and devotion to the Divine. The Vaishnavite saints known as Alvars were so intoxicated in the bliss of God-realization that they even sang in their songs, 'I don't want mukti!' They preferred that God be other than themselves.

"Enlightenment without God-realization," he said, "may manifest love and wisdom, but it does not manifest power." This surprised me. He continued: "In the past, God-realized beings have been able to manifest miracles, while merely enlightened beings have only succeeded in altering erroneous perceptions or giving the teachings of liberation, not actually liberating people. Miracles happened around them only occasionally."

In the past, people have become either enlightened or God-realized, but very rarely both. Bhagavan is doing something that has not been done before. He is bringing us the marriage between enlightenment and God-realization, the unity between wisdom and devotion. It is this unity that manifests as power, the power to heal and to transfer states of enlightenment. Collectively, it is the power to create new worlds. We become the doorway to eternity!

A couple of days later, we went through an empowerment ceremony, where we were given a deeksha empowering us to give deeksha to others. Every time we place our hands on people's heads with intent, Amma and Bhagavan's energies would flow through us to heal, give peace of mind, or transfer enlightenment, depending on what is requested. I felt an immense gratitude as the ceremony progressed. It was the fulfillment of a longing to help humanity, which I had experienced ever since I was a child. When I read the Gospels as a teenager, I had been profoundly affected by the Book of Acts, in which the disciples of Jesus are "baptized by the Holy Spirit" to teach, heal, and perform miracles in the name of Christ.

I felt the same excitement in my soul as I imagined those disciples must have felt. Even more, perhaps, for this was the first time in human history that an avatar had incarnated who could actually transfer states of enlightenment to people—not just some people, but anyone who asked, with no strings attached! It was with awe that I realized that we were being asked to serve as extensions of his avataric presence in the world! We were individually blessed and given a *mala* as a symbol of Bhagavan's empowerment.

Immediately after the empowerment ceremony, we were given a deeksha. It was quite gentle, and I didn't have any major insights or experiences. We were told that it was a stabilization deeksha, designed to better integrate our state of enlightenment. The state has continued to deepen since then.

12.

Life After Enlightenment

Once, I had seen enlightenment as the end of my spiritual journey, the ultimate in human attainment. Now, I see that it is merely a new beginning. Consciousness has its own intelligence, its own cycles, and it is an endless journey of discovery.

What happens after the peak experiences stabilize? What does "normal" reality look like afterward? How is this different from my normal reality before enlightenment?

It is very difficult to gauge this change. I don't have much of a reference point anymore for my life prior to enlightenment. I try to think of what it was like to engage in human drama, and I just can't seem to go there. It is as though I woke up from a dream, and realized that although the dream reality was similar to waking reality, it was also very different.

At the same time, many things are the same. Just because I am not identified with a fixed self does not mean that I am some blob of consciousness floating around without an identity. I am still Kiara, with the same memories and the same blend of personalities, except that Kiara is no longer caught up in a treadmill of mental chatter and noise. I was already pretty much at peace with myself; already felt a lot of fulfillment in my work and relationships, and already felt that I was contributing a lot to the world: These things have not changed.

What has changed are my motivations. I am no longer struggling to be at peace, struggling to make relationships work, or struggling to change the world. It is, rather, an effortless way of life, based on the recognition that I am not in charge, that there is a divine perfection at play that is far bigger than my capacity to understand or control it, and that I am simply a hollow reed in service to this divine play.

The most notable change is the profound silence I experience throughout the day. The silence does not depend on external factors. It does not matter whether I am talking or writing or thinking or meditating. This silence is here to stay. It is the undercurrent of everything I now experience.

I have had a practice of meditating with the sound current, a tone experienced inside the head, which takes you into deeper states of consciousness. I had never been able to get beyond a certain depth, however. Now, in this profound silence, the sound current takes me into vast realms of joy.

I experience this silence as an absence of mental static. It is as though I exchanged a pair of crackling speakers for a studio-quality sound system. When I pay attention to this silence, it opens up the door to an endless creative flow. I started writing this book soon after my enlightenment process ended. The creative energy came through strongly, and I followed it, writing for hours at a time without tiring or pausing. Within a week, most of it was written. The silence was the source of this inspiration, and I felt an immense joy in expressing from it. I could understand now what Simon and Garfunkel meant when they titled a song "The Sounds of Silence"!

Our guide was forever reminding me that enlightenment is nothing but disengaging from the mind. The silence is the sound of this disengagement!

Instead of a single, continuous stream of identity, I now experience myself as bubbles of consciousness, rising and falling, with the silence underneath. An emotion or a thought comes up, remains for a while, and then disappears into the silence. Another emotion or thought comes up, remains for a while, and again disappears into silence. When the mind is needed, it is extremely focused and efficient. When it isn't needed, I return into the silence.

These bubbles of consciousness could be anything. It certainly does not mean that I am free from frustration or anger or irritation or hurt. Before enlightenment, I had a misconception that enlightenment means instant saintliness. No, all these emotions still come and go as before. The difference is that where previously that would become my identity, now I simply watch them come up, and watch them disappear. I no longer feel the need to judge them or myself. I am no longer identified with saintliness.

Life continues around me. Things happen that are distressing, situations that I'd rather avoid. My senses are more acute, so I am more susceptible to problems with noise and pollution, but strangely, I notice that although I still have preferences, I don't have the same reactive emotional charge around these things. Whether it is noisy streets or complaining neighbors, family squabbles or world events, I notice a sense of equanimity. Sometimes I get upset about things, but it is like watching someone else falling back on an old habit. As soon as I become aware of it, it begins to change. I notice that I have more choices, and am not controlled by moods and emotional swings. The ability to disengage from human drama seems to keep growing, although disengagement is not always instant or easy.

Another misconception about enlightenment that I once had was that there would be an instantaneous flowering of psychic gifts and inner vision, or that I would forever dwell in cosmic consciousness. This has not been so. I notice, however, that my craving for these things has disappeared with the recognition that all things come in their appropriate season. With the narrow identity of a fixed self gone, I see that I am a channel for the entire universe to flow through, and that these gifts and states will come and go as needed. There is no sense of lack here, no sense that I have to hold onto something, even the highest states of *samadhi*.

There is no more trying to meditate. Or, to say it differently, all my life is now a meditation. Much of my need to meditate earlier was to stop the chatter in my mind so that I could attune to the vastness. This is my normal state now, and I am able now to experience as deep a state of consciousness in two minutes of stillness than after an hour of meditation before enlightenment. Yes, there is a lot further to go, especially as I observe some of the ecstatic states that the guides go into on a regular basis, but I no longer crave these states. This moment is profound enough!

I notice an increase in synchronicity. Although I have noticed synchronicities in my life for a long time, I am aware now that synchronicity is an outcome of being intimately connected with the universe. With the fixed self gone, the universe flows through. When the universe flows through, ordinary human limits are transcended. All of creation participates in responding to your every request. And why not? Every desire is now an expression of consciousness creating through you!

I have become aware that the soul is nothing but a focal point for this universal flow of consciousness. Before enlightenment, I conceived of the soul as a higher self, fixed somehow, and belonging to me. Now, there is no "me" to belong to, because there is no "other" to separate from. In experiencing life from the perspective of soul, I see that there is no fixed soul, just as there is no fixed self. As the yogis have always said, "Atman is Brahman," meaning that the individual soul is not separate from the universal soul, or God. I am not the same as God, but we are not separate. We are two aspects of the same reality.

With this recognition, I experience far less resistance to life. I am part of a river that sweeps along everything in its path as it flows toward its destination. I am no longer pushing it, so it no longer has to push me back. Sometimes I go back to trying to do things the old way, planning for the future and attempting to direct my life in certain channels. The more I push, the more frustrating it gets, until I finally give up. Then, the universe begins to reveal its own plan, exquisitely better than anything I could create by myself!

It was interesting to leave Oneness University and notice a newspaper for the first time in weeks. I had been a political and environmental activist, aware of all the wrongs in the world and intent on getting people to see the truth. Somehow, I don't feel the need to change the world on the outer level anymore. I can see that human drama is an outcome of an evolutionary push that is forcing us to clean out our metaphysical closets, and I know that, despite all the evidence of our outer senses, our passage into the Golden Age is assured.

I realize that I am very much a beginner on this path. Shortly after my enlightenment, when Grace and I were invited to a darshan with Bhagavan, he told me that at some point, there would come a "dark night of the soul," where everything would drop away: all the good feelings, all the synchronicities, and even the sense of direct communion with God. "You won't even have the ability to create any kind of meaning in your life anymore," he said.

It would be akin to Christ's forty days of wrestling with Satan in the wilderness, and necessary in order to enter into more profound states of oneness with God. Right now, I am aware of a sweet glow surrounding the enlightened state, but in the dark night, I could feel as though I were going through hell. It is a necessary stage if I choose to clean out the unconscious mind; the unconscious mind, says Bhagavan, is our personal link to the ancient mind. Having cleaned this out, we become a Christ. It is what the ancient initiations in the Great Pyramid of Giza were designed to do.

Perhaps this dark night is what the Australian aborigines and shamans in various traditions refer to as dismemberment, in which a person's entire foundation of being is erased. Everything that once provided meaning disappears. This stage is necessary in order to disengage from the collective mind of humanity. It was from this state that Jesus was able to realize his mission. It is from this state that the critical mass of enlightened people will be able to move the rest of the world into enlightenment.

I remember sitting in a bookshop one day as a teenager, drawn to a book that spoke of the descent of the Holy Spirit after Jesus ascended from his physical body. There was a baptism of power, and the disciples were empowered to go out into the world and heal the sick, raise the dead, and cast out demons, just as Christ had done. "All these things you shall do, and even greater things than these," he said, "because I go unto the Father." Ever afterward, that was all I wanted to do, and I prayed that I, too, might become one of his disciples, that I, too, would receive this baptism of the Holy Spirit. I was so disappointed when I was told by well-meaning clergy that the age of miracles had passed away with Jesus.

Perhaps there is an ebb and flow to all cycles. I have seen that the age of miracles, if it ever really passed away, is once again here in our midst, and I am so grateful to be a tiny instrument in this vast plan for the liberation of all humanity.

There is a new humanity being birthed, a new earth arising in our midst. I pray that the winds of Creation inspire each of us toward this realization. May we each become an empty sky for the whole universe to blow through!

Winds of New Birth

I searched through the world's illusions and strife
For the pearl beyond price, for true meaning in life.
For long years I grappled with right and wrong,
Uncertainties and doubts, as I struggled along.
I read all the books, and in strange postures did bend,
Howled through the night for old traumas to end.
I suppressed all my passions, all earthly desire,
Sacrificed all to the Great Cosmic Fire.
Yet through all my struggles, it was clear to me
I never got closer to where I should be.
Thus I journeyed through life, I gave up my youth,
Grew old with my questing, still searching for Truth.
Until one day on my visioning rock
With painful clarity I knew I must stop.
I'd followed each rule, tried only to love,
Given up earth for heaven above.
Meditated for years, but still couldn't stop mind,
And deeper cravings were all I could find.
"Could it be," I asked in restless confusion
"That this search for the pearl is itself an illusion?"
A dangerous question—the conflict grew worse:
"Could it be that my seeking itself is a curse?"
Too old I was now, too set in mind's ways,
But my seeking was worthless, I saw through my daze.
"Yet to give up the search would surely be death—

So safe in illusion I will draw my last breath."
Then one day I met Bhagavan, and Amma, his wife—
Surely the grandest event of my life!
And suddenly was light, the heavens were riven.
A gold ball descended, the deeksha was given.
"Can a drowning man pull himself out by the hair?
Can mind discover stillness by running here and there?
Seeking brought you here, now the seeking 'self' must die.
Efforts cannot earn you grace, however hard you try!
Mukti avatar am I, come to give you this grace—
All who yearn for suffering's end—to live in life's embrace."
Gladly I heard the words, and gratefully received.
No longer slave to mind, my lifelong conflict ceased.
The seeker died, as did self; the cravings died, too—
No more Wind Rider now: Only the Wind blows through!

II

Other Experiences of Enlightenment

13.

Grace

In this section, I share other people's experiences of enlightenment. When I sent out a call for people to send me their enlightenment experiences, I was overwhelmed by the deluge I received. There were enough stories to compile an entire book! My task was difficult, but I finally chose six accounts to share, all from people I knew well. As you will see, each person's experience is unique. I begin this section with Grace's experience.

Grace had the privilege of being among the first group of Westerners to get enlightened. Amma's birthday is August 15, which also happens to be India's Independence Day and Sri Aurobindo's birthday. Shortly after August 15, 2003, tens of thousands of people gathered for a darshan with Amma and Bhagavan in Nemam, and Grace and I were among them. In the first experiment of this kind, Bhagavan decided to use the occasion to initiate the transfer of enlightenment to people in the crowd. I will let Grace speak for herself. She can be reached at grace@deekshafire.com.

How we came to Bhagavan's abode is, in itself, grace. Looking back, I can see his guiding hand throughout a period of months. One day in April, Kiara and I were having lunch in Auroville when two women, eating a large plate of fruit, sat down beside us. They had just come from Oneness University in south India and were filled with glowing enthusiasm about Bhagavan's dharma. We were intrigued, and thought we would perhaps go sometime before I had to leave India.

Shortly afterward, we received several e-mails from trusted friends in the United States, urging us to attend a healing arts gathering known as the Experience Festival. It was being held at Oneness University. When Kiara investigated, he was invited to speak, and we were both invited to attend. We had the honor of meeting Bhagavan in the first few days. I found him to be a pure delight! He was kind and funny and welcoming, yet embodied a quiet power and presence.

Later that week, we attended a mukti program. Within a couple of days of starting the course, we were taken as a group to Nemam for darshan with Amma and Bhagavan in honor of Amma's birthday. There were tens of thousands of people there, and as part of the group from the course, we were blessed to sit in front, where we remained for two darshans. During the first darshan, two male guides were moving through the crowd and placing their hands on people's heads, giving deeksha. I really didn't know what this was all about, but I observed carefully what was happening and felt that there was definitely more power coming through one of them. As I observed him, something within me said very powerfully, *I'm ready!* The guide, who was some distance away, looked at me, caught my eye, and nodded. He immediately changed his course through the crowd as if he had heard me, and was in front of me within a few minutes.

He placed one hand on Kiara's head and one on mine, pressing firmly for perhaps two or three minutes. I felt as though I were being hit by lightning, but in slow motion. The heat and electric charge built up until it was almost unbearable.

When he took his hand away, I was unable to move or open my eyes for about 40 minutes. Several large bumps appeared on my head that were extremely tender, and my whole head throbbed and buzzed. Luckily, they allowed us to stay for another darshan, because I was unable to see or move. Then, we took a taxi back.

I was very disoriented and nauseous, with a pounding head and surges of heat everywhere. I was barely able to walk, and totally unable to think. Back in our hut, I went directly to bed and fell fast sleep.

The next morning, I awoke to great peacefulness. I felt like a vast, still lake. It was not an empty stillness, but very fluid and alive, and filled with a quiet completeness and joy.

That morning before class, I stood in front of the *srimurti* (portrait) of Amma and Bhagavan in gratitude and reverence, when their eyes started to sparkle and move! Amma's eyes began to blink as I looked at her. I was amazed and looked around to see if anyone else could see this. I beckoned to Kiara to come and look, but he did not see me.

As we meditated later, a large opening came in my *ajneya* chakra, so big, dark, and visceral that I put my hand up to see if there was something pressing on my forehead. In this opening, I suddenly saw myself lying there on the floor, although my form was very different. I was a man with a gray beard dressed in white. I felt great feelings of love and familiarity. I knew that this was me without question, and said to myself in wonderment, *Oh! I am really that man!* Later, the guide told me that the man was Bhagavan, and the experience was to show me that he and I were one.

The next day in meditation, as we brought energy up through the chakras, it went through my crown and beyond. Several tubes of opalescent light rose from my crown chakra to a flat, elliptical disk some distance above my head. The disk was a beautiful opalescent color, silvery, golden, and pink, and very subtle; a rarefied, highly refined beauty and ethereal vibration.

The disk slowly began to rotate, very serene and beautiful. As it moved, beams of light radiated out from it. Some were large and powerful, others subtle and more fine. The beams spread out across the planet, and I could see the earth from space, a blue marble with an amorphous pink cloud of love fed by these beams, moving and undulating around and over the earth. I walked home feeling as though I were this rarified, fine, and delicate frequency in human form. My feet barely touched the earth, so light and delicate and beautiful was I.

A little later, I saw one of the guides and told him of my experience and that I thought I was seeing a new chakra. He explained that my chakra system had made its link with universal consciousness. He said that human beings were intended to be linked in this way, but had somehow become disconnected. Now that I had been reconnected, he said, I could become enlightened.

That evening, we were taken as a group to a darshan with Bhagavan. When we got there, Bhagavan told us, "I am going to do something we haven't done with Westerners before. We will be giving everyone the deeksha. Everyone will become enlightened, if not immediately, then within twenty-four hours, or forty-eight hours, or over the next few weeks or months. The seed of enlightenment will be planted."

I somehow knew definitively that it would be forty-eight hours for me. He explained about putting the guides into a high state of divine union, where they would transfer bliss to us. He said not to worry if they got a little noisy: They were simply going into states of ecstasy! We were to please keep our eyes closed.

As we sat there, I heard such tremendous laughter and sounds of joy from the dozen or so guides that I opened one eye and peeked as a female guide started giving deeksha to the woman next to me. I thought, *What has he given them?*

The guide was in a very high state of divine ecstasy, trembling and laughing, face skyward, cooing in bliss. Her face was one vast smile, and tears of joy were on her cheeks. When she gave deeksha to me, she hugged me, caressed me, and kissed my cheeks. When I touched her, she was like a faun trembling in my arms.

After her came five or six male guides giving deeksha. None had the impact of the first deeksha in Nemam, but the cumulative effect was immense and overpowering.

I "cooked" all night, with electrical surges of great heat coursing through my body. I had a splitting headache, great sensitivity to light, and disorientation. This continued all day and the next day, and when it began to diminish that evening, I said, "Bhagavan, you can finish me off. I'm ready!"

Immediately, the heat was turned up, and I began to cook in earnest. This continued with increasing intensity through the night and into the next morning. It was Sunday and everyone had left for another darshan in Nemam. The last thing I wanted was another deeksha given to the boiling pot within my head! We decided to go to our hut and have a quiet meditation while the group was in darshan. I was feeling so poorly that I lay down on the bed.

Then I heard a mighty rumble, like that of a freight train, which came in and around my body. The heat became unbearable: Every nerve ending was on fire. This freight-train energy rumbled up through my physical and subtle bodies, lifting me up off the bed as though I were a paper doll. The pounding of my heart was deafening, and my breathing came faster and faster.

As the energy reached my heart, tears flowed silently from my eyes, the joy surged, and my face became an immense smile from ear to ear. My neck arched and my head went back as the energy shot through my crown and beyond to the "bliss body." I went into a state of ecstasy, laughing and crying uncontrollably, my body being tossed around like a limp rag doll.

During this time, I had only two awarenesses. First, *It's happening!* And second, *Thank you, Bhagavan.*

I saw Bhagavan's face smiling at me through the whole experience. He was right: It was a purely neurobiological event. Although I was a mystic, I saw no wondrous mystical visions. I simply felt and heard the tremendous energy tearing through my body. When the laughing subsided, I had no control of my body. My arms and legs didn't work. I was unable to speak. I was in a place of pure delight with everything.

My husband was watching all this, and he gently touched my aura with his fingertip. I shivered and giggled. Every slight touch, movement, or sound was immense. After perhaps an hour and a half, I was able to sit up. Looking at him blissfully, I tentatively touched his nose with my finger and laughed. I was looking at the world through the eyes of a baby, awestruck by everything. Noses are such a source of fun for a little baby, the funniest thing you can imagine!

Simultaneously, I was an immense consciousness, vast and wise and observing in wonder. . .

Some time later, we were outside. The trees looked endless, and my husband so tall. With the motor skills of a young child, eating was interesting; sometimes I missed my mouth completely. At the same time, this immense new presence that was "me," was everywhere and nowhere.

Kiara called a guide, and he came, laughing and saying, "She's got it! It's the classical enlightenment." That day, I progressed to about two and a half years old, and that night, everything became overpowering. Light, sounds, and smells were causing me intense pain. Kiara was concerned and consulted a guide, who said, "She's going through some sensory changes. By tomorrow, she will stabilize."

The next day, I felt better, and about four years old. Four is a wonderful age. Everything is an adventure! The following day, I was eight years old. That evening, we went to see Bhagavan. I felt like a little girl. I remember when he turned his full attention on me, it seemed as though the whole universe were smiling on me with infinite patience and love, welcoming me. Bhagavan said to me, "We know each other now, and we are friends. If you ever need me, just call me, and I will come." What a wonderful thing for God to say when you are eight years old—or eighty for that matter!

The next day, we had to leave for Bangalore. I was reluctant to go. I liked my little house and my little bed with pink sheets. When we left, the sky looked so big and people seemed so noisy. In India, sometimes buses can be a nightmare: crowded and hot, with blaring music. My bus was a blessing—silent and dark, and I had a seat to myself. As we drove through villages, I watched through the open window in a state of bliss. There were rainbows around all the lights. I was in fairyland or maybe heaven. Perhaps when you are eight, they are the same.

We arrived in Bangalore. I felt as though I were a small Bhagavan walking around. No more was I "myself." Kiara's brother, a genius in computer engineering, asked me a few days later, "What is enlightenment?" I said, "I don't know. I don't know anything and it's okay." He said with great seriousness, "I think that's what enlightenment is."

Since then, I have had seven months of integration, the last three at Oneness University. There have been new peak experiences, new revelations, and new ways of seeing the world and relating to people. It has been a steady progression, although sometimes it seems as though I regress. When that happens, it seems to be a gathering up and bringing forward of something deep that needs to be changed. As I begin to observe it—no blame, no guilt, and no denial—it transforms itself, sometimes in a matter of seconds, and dissolves into a high state of gratitude and bliss.

Bhagavan says that any emotion, authentically experienced, becomes bliss. This is true. It is our refusal to see something, or our continuing to judge something that we don't want to acknowledge that keeps us stuck and causes us pain. If we just look at it with kindness and say, "Oh yes, I see that's there," it goes away almost magically, leaving bliss in its wake. It has done its work, which is to wake us up, so it is free to become bliss, too.

I know now what it is like for babies when they are born, when their senses and nervous systems are completely open, how wondrous is each perception of their world. How gently and lovingly they must be regarded, as they have come fresh from God. Bhagavan tells us that *babies are born enlightened.* What does that tell us about the importance of our realizing enlightenment as a species?

I remember how I felt when my children were born, not unlike being with Bhagavan and all the enlightened people. I was in bliss for the first nine months of my daughter's life, and realize now that I was in the presence of an enlightened being. But then I got caught up in the material world and the rat race of acquisition we call life in the affluent West, and didn't have time to just be with them. And then our beautiful children forget who they are, just as we did.

Bhagavan has come to return all of us to our natural state, the state of our childhood, the state of enlightenment. And enlightenment is just the beginning.

14.

Barry

Barry Martin is a close friend of mine from California. He and his partner, Karen, first pointed my way toward Bhagavan by forwarding me an Experience Festival newsletter, which inspired me to go to Golden City. I then invited them both to come and experience what was going on there. Barry experienced a five-day enlightenment process March 1–5, 2004. They returned again in February 2005 for the twenty-one-day process. I will let Barry report his experience in his own words.

The journey with Bhagavan began an eternity ago, when we all came into embodiment to realize the fullness of the Divine here. In this lifetime, I first heard of him through an Experience Festival newsletter. Last year, my partner, Karen Anderson, came across an article about the Experience Festival in the Global Village newsletter. She immediately felt that our dear friends Kiara and Grace, who were visiting India, might be interested in learning more about this upcoming festival.

Kiara and Grace not only became involved in the festival, but also went to see Bhagavan and attended a deeksha. When I heard that Grace had become enlightened, I wanted to know more. When I began to meditate with Bhagavan's picture, I felt a very high frequency of golden white light pouring in, and received the strong knowing that he was somehow my next—and final—step.

Beginning in 1986, I had many kundalini awakenings and oneness experiences. I resided in the oneness most of the time, and yet emotional patterns would still arise, and the veils of the separated mind would temporarily engulf me. After nearly twenty years of inner work, a number of patterns still remained, and although they grew ever less powerful, they nonetheless continued to be a source of suffering.

I came to realize that something was amiss in the neurological structure of my brain. I did many brain clearings, using numerous inner and outer technologies, throughout the years, yet I never found the switch to turn off the ego's control over my consciousness. I knew that I had to go to India to see Bhagavan when I read an article in which he said that enlightenment is a neurobiological process, and that he was like a surgeon who changed the brain structure function, resulting in illumination. The light went on! I made plans to attend the next Enlightenment Process. I could hardly wait to receive the deeksha, which, I had read, changes the brain structure and establishes the state of enlightenment.

Powerful shifts in consciousness began to occur as soon as Karen and I arrived at Oneness University. I felt as though I were being processed and worked on by Bhagavan 24/7. The first really powerful experience occurred during the *samskara shuddi* (an emotional clearing process). After a particularly potent catharsis, an energy descended through my crown chakra, and I felt my body dissolve. The process was over and everyone was getting up, yet I could not make my body move. There was no place where I could find the connection between personal will and the body. In fact, I couldn't even sense any personal will present in this state of empty oneness. As I lay there, there was no fear, just a curious observing of this state, and a detached wondering whether someone would come and notice me lying there eventually, or if I might go to the bathroom in my pants or what.

After maybe forty-five minutes, a fly landed on my arm, and involuntarily the body decided to move on its own. It became clear that the body is conscious and capable of doing everything it needs to do in order to convey the soul through life. Such a letting go came with this realization! I could relax and let the body do it all. Then, I found the body getting me up off the floor into a sitting position. Gradually, it decided to walk me out the door to experience the magnificence of the sunlight. To this day, the body continues to be orchestrated through a superconscious connection, and I, in a way, am just along for the ride, yet one with all that is unfolding.

In another samskara shuddi session, I became aware of a sense of sadness about the severe damage I had done to my left index finger when I cut it to the bone with a hacksaw in the spring. All the nerves were severed and had not grown back, so I had become resigned to living life with no feeling in the tip of this very important finger. It was annoying when things would slip out of my hand, and the loss of this sensuous connection when touching myself, others, and the many wonderful things of life created this sense of sadness and loss.

In the moment that I embraced the sadness in its fullness, and acknowledged the desire to have it healed, I felt the descent of the presence of Bhagavan again, down through the crown chakra and into the arm and finger. Instantaneously, I realized that I could have feeling back in the finger. Joy, gratitude, and reverence for the love and power of Bhagavan filled my heart, along with an all-encompassing love and desire to see us all totally happy and joyful. I also realized that I was not able to fully open to this magnificence, and thus not all the feeling in the finger was restored—but it continues to gain more feeling by the day.

The deeksha was the crown jewel of the Oneness University experience, and the most pivotal event of my lifetime. When Bhagavan arrived, I immediately knew that my spiritual path had come to an end. As I watched him empower the guides, my tears of overwhelming gratitude flowed freely. By that point, I couldn't walk anymore, so I crawled up to the deeksha line. As the guides placed their hands upon my crown chakra, I felt overwhelming bliss. With each transmission, the feelings of love and joy dissolved all sense of "me."

When I looked into the eyes of our guides, I was looking at the only self that exists. I experienced a sense of oneness—a complete emptiness—yet a fullness of such peace and happiness that it cannot be adequately described, only experienced. Drunk on divine bliss, I staggered away from the deeksha line, waving to everyone as they laughed with joy at my seemingly drunken state. As I lay on the floor, I felt complete, liberated. My heart knew that my long search was, finally, complete.

A feeling of love and peace and gratitude to Bhagavan that words cannot do justice to grows continuously within me to this day. The only desire I have is to deepen endlessly into this state, and to give my life to assisting others to experience it also.

~

Notes from the Year After the First Visit

In the days just after coming home from Golden City, what is most apparent is that the old patterns of reality orientation are gone. Sleep cycles and dietary preferences are constantly shifting. Sometimes I am up at 3 A.M., sleep all afternoon, and go to bed late. The next, day it's something different. Today, Karen slept twenty-four hours. This seems to be because the body needs to spend immense amounts of time and energy integrating the divine infusions. The body gets up and moves when it wants to; it cannot be moved with an act of mind or will, both of which are practically nonexistent.

The process continues to deepen, and dissolution is the main feature of my reality. The state induced by the deeksha seems quite solid. I have even played with it to see if it could be short-circuited. *No such possibility.* The continuous witness and experience of oneness is now my foundational reality. Discordant thoughts and feelings arise much less frequently, and there is practically no "charge" to them. They don't obscure awareness, because I have so little attachment to or identification with them.

Karen and I both experience times when our dovetailing patterns start to get triggered, but they pass across the sky of the mind without our becoming enmeshed in them. Occasionally, there is a sense of just how much what had previously had been the basis for suffering and separation has disappeared. Gone. *Thank God.* My sense of gratitude to the Divine is beyond expression. A state that I long yearned for, and intuited as a possibility, is now here—and so much more. And this is just the beginning.

⁓

During the remainder of 2004, there was a deepening in the state and also the sense of a very thin veil still present at times, only slightly obscuring the oneness state. Later in the year, a friend noticed how much energy Karen had coming out of her hands when he jokingly asked her to place her hands over his head. We were spontaneously guided to give each other deekshas a few weeks later, and we both experienced very powerful states, and were not functional afterward. We realized the deeksha energy was coming through spontaneously. Later, we gave deekshas to two friends, who both had powerful experiences and went through weeks of purification and consciousness shifts afterward. This further sparked our desire to return to Oneness University for the twenty-one-day process, in order to be empowered to give the deeksha and further deepen in the state.

Most of the twenty-one days was rather mild in its impact compared with the previous visit, which was a testimony to the state that we had earlier realized.

One important event occurred at dinner on the night before the course began. I was sitting across from Patrick, a Sweish devotee. He looked at me and said, "You are there. All that remains is to simply accept everything just as it is." I realized that I still had a subtle resistance to certain experiences. Today, after holding deeksha groups, I see this as possibly the most important thing to comprehend for those who want to awaken. The ego's pursuit of perfection is one of the great cul-de-sacs that keeps its illusory existence alive, thus posing a major impediment to realization.

The greatest gift of the twenty-one-day program occurred toward the end, at a time when I was enjoying the experience without any expectation of anything more occurring of major significance. Then, it happened. I was watching a video in which Bhagavan said two things, which initiated a major shift. "The search *is* the self [separate self], is suffering." Then he said, "Postponing awakening is the height of hypocrisy." Suddenly, I saw, as never before, the spiritual ego that I had spent so much of my life constructing. And, although I was considerably awakened, unconsciously, the ego was still using the search for higher, deeper, and more expansive states to continue its existence. This was not a new concept, but the living experiential reality of it hit me like a ton of bricks. I found every part of my being calling out for deliverance from this embedded pattern of identity. I prayed to Bhagavan for assistance, turning the whole matter over to him.

Then, the shift happened. I heard a very quiet voice say, *The search is over.* A peace beyond understanding descended, and I felt the subtle remains of the gnawing hole in the center of the soul, which spawns all seeking, disappear. I knew with absolute certainty that I was home, in the place that I had intuitively known existed, which I had always hoped I would arrive at. Yet it did not feel like going anywhere at all. It was the place where I always had been, but just hadn't been fully conscious of. The shift was so incredibly subtle, yet so totally profound.

After a few minutes of basking in this indescribable feeling of absolute wholeness and peace, the desire to share this with beloved Karen arose. I looked across the room to where she was sitting and found her staring directly at me. As our eyes met, it was instantly apparent that she had arrived at the same place that I was experiencing. My joy, my happiness, and my gratitude were profound. After the session ended, we walked across the room toward each other. As we touched, she said the first words: "The search is over"—the very same words that I had heard!

If there was even the slightest shred of doubt remaining within, it was totally shattered then. We hugged and cried and rejoiced, and to this day, we still do. Despite the seeming dissonance of the world, this state of peace, joy, and happiness is beneath, through, around, and beyond it all, for it is our native state of being. Thoughts and feelings still arise, but they have no place to stick. They glide across the sky of awareness like clouds in an empty sky. Sometimes we still experience a fog, but it is rare and fleeting.

Everything seems clear, without conflict or mental effort. This state is not an extraordinary or even transcendental state. It simply is, what is. And it has stood up to the intensity of dealing with the death of a dear friend and close neighbor, and the death process of Karen's father, not to mention the everyday issues of sick pets, high-pressure jobs, illness, and all the other challenges of third-dimensional existence. The real test was a dark night of the soul that Karen went through just after returning. Despite the intensity of the dark emptiness that she experienced, the base level of the oneness state was there. Whatever her experience, it was all held within that state.

I, too, have gone through times of having deeper samskaras being released, but again, there is no real impact on the oneness. It is seen as part of an ongoing process that continues until we graduate from our sojourn with third-dimensional physical existence.

I now know that this is what enlightenment and oneness really are: simply returning to that "empty-yet-full" native state of being, in which peace, joy, and a sense of completeness are the foundation of existence—and in which everything simply is just as it is. It is not a goal to be achieved or an end point in the journey, but the very truth and foundation of being itself, which deepens on forever into infinity.

15.

Karen

Without the inspiration of my dear friend Karen Anderson, I would not have met Bhagavan! She and Barry live close to Mt. Shasta, California, a magical spot of spiritual pilgrimage for many. With a background of spiritual·psychotherapy, they are both committed to taking this work to the next level of support for people experiencing the deeksha. Karen can be reached at soulspace@cot.net.

Karen's account highlights the contrast between the intensity of the earlier days described here, and the quiet, relaxed atmosphere prevalent now. It is like a volcano, which having erupted initially with great intensity, continues to bring forth a fire in a gentle, fluid way. As the morphogenetic field of enlightenment continues to get stronger, Bhagavan no longer feels it necessary to personally oversee the deeksha process and is content to play a less visible role. As participants at these intensives are empowered to become deeksha givers themselves, each becomes, in his or her own unique way, a channel for these same avataric energies.

It's early in the summer of 2003. Sitting at my desk, my eyes light up at an e-mail announcing an upcoming Experience Festival in India. Our dear friends Kiara and Grace are in

India, and an unmistakable inner excitement tells me that I must send them the information about this festival right away.

A few days later, we receive an e-mail from Kiara. He is not only planning to attend the festival, he's been invited to join the teaching faculty! Weeks pass, and another e-mail arrives from Kiara, bearing stupendous news. Grace has entered into an enlightened state! The festival, as it turns out, was held at the Oneness University, where a man named Bhagavan claims that he can give the gift of enlightenment to people through something called deeksha. During a public deeksha, or transmission of the state of oneness, Grace has been catapulted into a state that most of us have been dreaming about for decades!

"Amazing things are happening here," Kiara asserts. "You might want to come over and check it out for yourselves." He goes on to tell us that Bhagavan says that enlightenment is not a spiritual phenomenon, but a neurobiological event. When certain changes happen in the brain, enlightenment naturally follows.

Hearing this, Barry is ecstatic. "This is what I've been waiting for!" he exclaims. "I *knew* the key had to be in the brain! I've tried all kinds of spiritual practices and meditations and therapeutic techniques, but certain mental and emotional patterns still persist. I've had the feeling that they needed to somehow be unlocked in the brain, but I didn't know how to go about it. This is exactly what I've been looking for!"

Kiara and Barry have been soul brothers ever since they met, nearly a decade ago. When one speaks, the other listens, and listens well. Now, Barry immediately begins planning the journey halfway around the world. I have never been particularly attracted to India, but Barry convinces me that this opportunity is too good to miss, and he feels certain that we both need to go.

Within days of stepping onto the soil of India, I have fallen under the spell of this ancient land and its vibrant people. We make our way to Oneness University, where we are greeted by an international welcoming committee of young women with the clearest eyes I've ever seen. Yes, something is going on here, and I can't wait to find out more.

Our classes begin, and the young disciples of Bhagavan who teach them are as calm and self-possessed a group of beings as I've ever encountered. Yet they retain their individuality in delightful ways. One loves to tease us about our concepts of enlightenment: "Do you think that you will leave here with a halo around your head?" Another insists, "We are no different from you. We have all the same thoughts and feelings. The only difference is that in us, there is no place for them to stick." Oh, how I long to have a Teflon-coated brain, as these ever-peaceful guides do!

After days of emotional cleansing and purification, accompanied by lecture sessions stressing the need to release all ideas about enlightenment and simply let it happen, we are finally ready for our deeksha. Three hundred of us are seated on the floor of a great hall, awaiting Bhagavan's arrival. When he enters the room, an aura of absolute composure and peace radiates from him as he strolls to the stage. He answers a few questions from the audience in a way that leaves no doubt in my mind that I am in the presence of an enlightened being. I marvel at my good fortune to be in this room, where the very atmosphere is charged with exultation.

Suddenly, it is time for the deeksha. One by one, the male guides approach Bhagavan with arms outstretched, palms facing up. Bhagavan places his hands above theirs, without touching them, for no more than a second. The energetic transmission is so intense that each of them goes limp and has to be escorted, if not carried, to his position sitting at the edge of the stage.

Each female guide then goes before Bhagavan in the same way. When they receive the energy, most immediately begin laughing uncontrollably—and contagiously. I find myself dropping into a stillness that only deepens as those around me are carried away with cosmic glee.

Now, the deeksha begins. The women will pass beneath the hands of the five or six female guides, as the men receive deeksha from as many male guides. I watch as dozens of men and women walk up, one by one, to the line of deeksha givers in the front of the room. As they place their hands on each person's head, I feel as though I, too, am receiving an energy transmission along with each one. The joy of witnessing so many beings lifted into their true magnificence fills me with gratitude for having been brought to this amazing place. There is Barry, looking as drunk as a sailor, leaning on the arm of a helper as he grins and waves to those of us still waiting our turn, as if to say, *This will soon be yours.*

And now it is my turn. As I take my place before the first guide, someone whispers, "Look into their eyes." And I do, before each of these extraordinary young women places her hands atop my head. With one or two, I seem to be gazing into infinity: Not the slightest residue of a personal self remains in those fathomless depths. In the eyes of others, I see the absolute knowing that all is taken care of, forever. As I reach the end of the line, I notice that, unlike many before me, my body still seems capable of walking. Grace escorts me to my place on the floor, and I lie down.

And there I remain for the next few hours—or eons—all sense of residing in a physical body having totally disappeared. Pure consciousness is all that remains. There is no "I": no thought, no feeling, no anything localized. What is present is vastness—without quality, without attribute. Floating in vastness, as vastness.

In this state of pure being, there is nothing to do and no one to do it. There is not even anyone who could possibly think this thought. Only now, as I write, is it possible to put words to the experience, and they are a distant shadow of a reality far more vibrant than anything this consciousness had previously experienced. In this empty-yet-full vibrancy I simply *am*, for a length of time that shall ever remain a mystery.

This state continues for some time longer, in the timeless expanse of pure being. Eventually, the eyes slowly and effortlessly open, and they notice that the room is nearly empty of people. I look around. Ah, the incredible, impermanent beauty of this realm! Tears flow, but there is no one crying. Joy arises, replaced by peaceful stillness, which segues into the thought that it might be nice to lie down on my bed, back in the dorm.

After some time, the body, of its own accord, slowly rises. After another eternity, it finds itself back in the dorm, and collapses onto the bed, where it remains until morning. Upon awakening, the body seems perfectly capable of doing whatever is necessary—but the senses still operate in slow motion. Even the minutest experience—picking up a fork, washing the hands, or acutely sensing the unique expression of life in each person walking by—seems to take place in a surreal realm. I move, act, respond—but there is no "me" doing any of it!

In the next days, I slowly become more and more functional, yet an undercurrent of something very different is always present. I feel altered in a major way, and a sense of inner quiet is ever present, right behind whatever is taking place in the outer world. There is little to say, and little desire to say it; and the pervasive feeling of calm, quiet happiness is beyond anything I've ever experienced. Gratitude rises up throughout the day, and I can hardly believe my good fortune in being brought to this place to receive the blessings of the deeksha.

Barry's consciousness, too, has been undergoing a similarly radical rearrangement. When, in a couple of days, we leave Oneness University to travel throughout south India, we find that nothing seems to have the power to upset us in any way. When we learn that our train will be four hours late, we simply sit down and relax, thoroughly enjoying sitting on a bench in the train station, watching the passing show. The heat plasters our clothing to our backs, but it's simply heat and sweat and rumpledness. Everything simply is what it is, and there is no desire on our parts to have it different. We feel freed of the heavy burden of preferences, delighted with what we find wherever we go.

Back in the United States, we find ourselves needing tremendous amounts of rest. Our sleep cycles take us on a wild ride: We might need two hours of sleep—or we might need twenty-four. We feel tremendous changes taking place in our brains, accompanied by a host of sensations, ranging from sharp, stabbing pains to diffuse pressure to sensations just beneath the skin. We bless it all and continually ask Amma and Bhagavan to bring us into a state of perfect peace and oneness. Already our lives have been forever changed; and we rest in the awareness that the process, along with our states of awareness, will continue to deepen.

Within a few months, Kiara writes to tell us that it is now possible to go through a longer program in India and receive the ability to give deekshas to people. "Is there anything that we'd rather do with the rest of our lives?" we ask each other.

Kiara says that Bhagavan formerly referred to as Kalki now wishes to be known simply as Bhagavan. He has no desire to be the focus of it all: He is simply a gateway for each person to connect with his or her own antaryamin presence, or inner divinity. Although I have never felt drawn to having a guru, I feel a tremendous love for this being whose eyes sparkle with joy.

A year after our first visit to Golden City, we return for the twenty-one-day program. The first few days of the program center on emotional cleansing and purification, in preparation for the core of the program: immersion into states of oneness that we will someday transfer to others through the deeksha. Teachings alternate with meditations and deekshas.

Each day, the guide leads us in a group meditation called the *ananda* mandala, in which we sit in two huge circles, holding hands. The meditation consists of a systematic progression of breathing into each chakra and focusing our consciousness on each energy center in turn, starting at the base of the spine and culminating at the crown of the head. When the breathing process is complete, several guides travel around each circle to give us a deeksha.

During our first ananda mandala deeksha, I experience the third eye opening into a vast field of brilliant, deep blue. It feels as if the top of my skull has come off and is now wide open to this infinite expanse of dazzlingly blue space. Living streams of gold extend out into space, framing the indigo sky-field in brilliant contrast. I rest in the splendor, filled with gratitude.

My eyes are drawn to the woman sitting beside me. How incredibly precious her face, her very being! Tears stream down my cheeks as I behold the divinity shining through those eyes looking back at me in amazement. The tears continue as I behold all the unbelievably beautiful beings, so precious in their every movement. Have I ever really seen anyone before? The splendor of it all is nearly more than I can handle: I am overcome with the glory.

Throughout the rest of the program, each day seems to intensify and ground the state of oneness. And although Barry and I rarely communicate, preferring to maintain silence, during one morning's presentation we share a moment of realization that lets us know our paths are exactly parallel. The guide has often reminded us that there truly is no self, just a collection of personalities. On this morning, he is telling us that because there is no self, there can be no seeker—and furthermore, because enlightenment is our true nature, there is nothing to seek! *The search is over*, I think, as elation floods my being. I look over at Barry, who "happens" to be looking right at me from his spot across the room. A huge grin lights up his face, and the light of crystal clear awareness shines from his eyes. When we meet after class, his first words are, "The search is over!"

The mind's incessant questioning ceases: There is no one left who wants to ask anything. I float in the eternal now, empty of all concepts, happy to rest in infinity. After our initiation, it is time to leave Oneness University and go out into the world as deeksha givers. When we return to the United States, I learn that my beloved father has been diagnosed with cancer. Within weeks, our dear neighbor dies. Childhood patterns and wounds reemerge, and I feel engulfed in a dark night that is every bit as intense as the exultant states were at Oneness University.

Bhagavan said that every one of us would, at some point, go through a dark night of the soul. It is remarkable to experience no resistance to the process: no thoughts of wishing it were different or hoping it will pass quickly or preferring one state to another. Everything simply is what it is, and there is absolute faith and trust that it is serving a purpose, or it wouldn't be happening. For decades I have inwardly heard, *You are being prepared for a time when large numbers of people will be in crisis.* I assume that this is yet another part of that preparation, and submit to it.

Shortly afterward, Barry and I are guided to offer a seven-month program to provide ongoing support to those awakening into oneness. We carefully observe the various stages that group members pass through, along with the permanent changes they are experiencing. Group members report less mental chatter. Some find the everyday affairs of life unfolding far more smoothly and effortlessly. Many report relief from the perfectionism of their egos, greater self-acceptance, and greater freedom from the personality patterns that formerly dominated their lives. For some, a quiet undertone of reasonless joy and happiness is now present. Fewer and fewer ideas, concepts, and beliefs separate them from the direct, moment-to-moment experience of life.

Most, if not all, group members appear to be enjoying the first stages of enlightenment. The witness state is growing more solid and imperturbable. Events and circumstances that would have been upsetting in the past are now accepted with little or no resistance. Feelings are allowed, not squelched, and because they are simply felt and accepted, they pass through with little residue.

Many have passed through the dark night of the soul, to a lesser or greater extent. Yet, looking around the group after several months, we see shining eyes and radiant faces: the true Self beaming out into the world. We listen to stories of breakthroughs in situations that once looked hopeless. Body language expresses a new level of comfort: a radical acceptance of what is, a growing compassion for self and others, and a level of trust previously only dreamed of. Workplaces are altering; relationships are being reborn; and new healing gifts are coming through.

Everywhere, hearts are flowering, minds are quieting, and a sense of oneness with self, others, and life is replacing separation. *We are so, so blessed.* And the journey has only begun.

16.

Mitchell

Grace and I met Mitchell Jay Rabin and his partner, Rena Majeed, shortly after the Experience Festival in February 2004. We immediately developed a close friendship with Mitchell and Rena, as did Barry and Karen. Mitchell lives in New York, and hosts a television show called *A Better World* (see www. abetterworld.net), dedicated to bringing healing and enlightenment to the planet. He and Rena participated in the five-day enlightenment process on March 1–5, 2004. Mitchell can be reached at mjr@abetterworld.net.

I had the golden opportunity to meet with Bhagavan and then to conduct an interview with him for *A Better World*, an educational TV program in New York, which I have hosted since 1993. This gave me a unique moment in which to get to know this amazing being. The interviews went extremely well: He was relaxed, the embodiment of kindness, warm-hearted, and simply a pleasure to be with. He also wanted to discuss the "world situation" with me and come up with solutions to the most agonizing of problems. It was gratifying to have time with this amazing, nurturing soul.

Meeting with Bhagavan was, in itself, a taste of awakening, but the enlightenment process was where I really experienced my own "splendor and fullness of being." Everything that would have been considered happening outside me was now happening inside me. There was no separation! The lights were turned on! I was in an utterly awakened state. The laughter and crying of others near me were happening inside me.

"I" was no longer the "I" as I knew "I" in any ordinary way, but the "I" that I knew in the depths of my bones. It was the realest "I" going.

We were touched by the hands of a few guides, after they had become visibly ecstatic by what appeared to be the simple viewing of Bhagavan and Amma's srimurti (photograph). But who knows, really, what induces such divine intoxication? All I know is that when they touched me, and sprinkled a few drops of blessed water on our heads, my reality changed. I went through this experience about six times. Truly, half of those were mild shifts. And the other half? Ecstatically poignant.

All experience was direct, totally rich, and fluid. There was also no separation among any idea of God, God itself, and "myself." I most immediately discovered this when, in the midst of ecstasy in gazing at the sky, I exclaimed, "Thank God for all this!" By thanking God, I was thanking everything equally, including "myself." There was no difference. This is when I knew that the Awakened Self was what was present.

It was as though the lights simply got turned on. I was in a reality in which all was one, and this was the natural course of things. I felt so alive! Until then, oh, I was alive to some extent, and indeed, more alive than many, but now, the deeper, higher Self got turned on, and I saw from the place where all was connected.

I was in the truth state, in harmony with all. It was the state from which teachings flow forth. I felt that I could get rid of all of my spiritual, books, because now I could write them myself. To have them would be redundant. I recognized that having them and reading them was a compensation for what I hadn't been in touch with inside myself. And I have compassion for this unawakened condition, God knows! In the awakened state, this whole perception of life is the book itself.

A part of my brain, mostly dormant until then, had gotten stoked, prodded, awakened by the deeksha. As Bhagavan says, this is a neurobiological process. I wholly agree. Our brains and nervous systems are hardly used. It is a truism that we use only 5 percent of our brains, right? Until now, that is. Through this process of deeksha, I now know something more, at least a bit more, about that other 95 percent. Within it is the treasure trove of ourselves. Not more book learning, not more concepts, but the domain of knowing: a place of spontaneous love and insight; of abiding, unconditional sisterly and brotherly regard and deep seeing; of compassion and wisdom.

I gained, through the masterful touch of Bhagavan, access to the rest of the brain, the nervous system, and, indeed, my true energy field. He helped me gain access to myself. But this self isn't me in any ordinary sense. This self is the same self of all beings: It is divine. To say "I am That" makes inherent, organic sense. My ordinary sense of self was not to be found anywhere. And at the same time, the words of Bhagavan echoed: "Six billion souls, six billion different enlightenments."

There remains a distinct personal blueprint, like an individual flower of a species that is now expressing this reality in its own unique way. It is an abiding in peace, in love, in knowing, and in presence. Call it God, call it Cosmic Joy! It doesn't matter. It is what it is, and it is the stuff of reality that is our true Divine Self. Tears of gratitude flowed sometimes, and heads bowed in grace at other times; at still other times, I heard peals of blissful laughter. Such was my experience.

In my life, I had ingested sacred plants, practiced tai chi and chi kung, and been involved in the Gurdjieff work and Buddhist and Taoist meditation practices for years. All of this had opened the doors to my consciousness, so that the terrain I entered after the deeksha was already quite familiar. This was not new territory, but no less wondrous. The sacred drink of the Amazonian sect Santo Daime, in particular, seemed to prepare the way well.

I was amused to see the similarities between the two methods. Bhagavan said that the dimensions where neurological pathways in the brain have already been cut would be the first places the deeksha would guide one to and through. So there I was in the middle of south India, and I felt that I could as well have been in the jungles of the Amazon! But it was better than that, because the light kept shining and the experience came from an internal source. Catalyzed by a frequency outside myself, I became awakened to my inner self.

It was what I had always searched for.

In Golden City, this holy place for which we had spent many lifetimes preparing to come, this humble, still, intent being, Bhagavan, through his guides, touched us and awakened our consciousness into its appropriate divine place. The dream of lifetimes was coming to fruition. I went to India on an intuition and a hunch. I hadn't been there in seven years. My visits to other gurus, interesting and worthwhile as they had been, hadn't done it for me. There was no connection to speak of, and certainly no offer of enlightenment. Here, the power was being given away. Bhagavan says, "Be your own teacher. Take the deeksha; let your own enlightenment guide you. Then, if you want, go back to your own religion or practice or teacher, enlightened!"

These are the words of a master. He wants nothing but for this beautiful earth, and all of our playmates, our brothers and sisters, to be in our fullness as divine, joy-filled beings all the way to the core. You know, when you really look at the bio-chemistry, you see that the human organism is designed for the ongoing experience of joy, pleasure, bliss.

What's an endorphin? What are the skin and the senses? A fragrant, yellow-bursting flower? There's no escaping it: We are set up for bliss. But look at us. We've missed; we've totally missed the mark. We live instead in suffering. These are not new ideas to me, nor possibly to you. But now I'm living the truth of it. They are not just words. They are my reality.

So all the teachings I've ever listened to are now living in me. I was leafing through some old writings and came across a journal entry I made years ago. It pleaded with the heavens for enlightenment and the ability to wholly serve, with all my being, this precious planet, people, and universe. Similar pleas to the universe are scattered throughout my writings, dating back to my teenage years. Then, in one extraordinarily gentle "blow to the head," I was awakened to that reality!

Shakespeare was right: this world is a play. And this state of oneness, free from suffering or duality, simply plugs a person into the large cosmic electrical outlet, and everything assumes its rightful place. If everyone were enlightened, there would not be a world of war or environmental destruction or ten percent owning and controlling ninety percent of the world's resources: it simply wouldn't happen.

So do I see this process as a means of truly taking this planet to its next level? Enlightened government! Enlightened society! Organic farming! Water distribution! Music! Dance! Fun! No kidding! It's so simple that it boggles the minds of those committed to the complicated. Unwinding the damage will take a little time and doing, but it is doable. The vibration of all of us enlightened people will itself be a major force in the undoing of the imbalance.

How wonderful! I see hope, I see hope, I see hope! As sisters and brothers, we are literally one, and to hurt another is to hurt oneself. This is no longer an idea. When one awakens, it is real. The games of power and control cannot be sustained. They lose their power, and there's no lure in this realm. The material realm is joyous, but it is not a realm any longer of "power over," but "power with." From the view of Golden City, and my view being there, this is the way it is.

The world as we've constructed it—with all its institutions with regulations, religions with rules, societies with restrictions, and military might—looks mighty strange from this view. Where did we get so many odd ideas? And why did we institutionalize them all? Soon, we'll all be free!

With this feeling in my breast, with all of us feeling this, the world will be transformed. There is no question about it. The power of reality, of truth, will assert itself. It is happening, right now. It is so powerful. There are powers at play far beyond anything we now know. As one vast ripple effect, hundredth-monkey style, once the first few thousand are enlightened, the rest of humanity will open like flowers. And the world as we know it today, with its wars, environmental destruction, and human pillage, will cease to be. It will simply cease to be.

The peak of deeksha shifts. It does not remain in full. What follows remains beautiful. There is a permanent shift in the energy field; and the shift in one's perceptions can be called upon by observing the drama of daily living, and while being wholly in it, watching it. And the flower-opening of humanity will be upon us in no time. Thank you, dear Bhagavan and Amma, for catalyzing in me my truest Self and empowering me to serve sentient beings in a higher way. Blessings to all!

17.

Patricia

Patricia Resch (worldpeaceby2012@yahoo.com) is a very special friend from Mt. Shasta, California. This following account was written in September 2005, immediately after her twenty-one-day process in August. The twenty-one-day programs are being continually updated; Patricia's story highlights some of the changes made within the past year. It is expected that once the Oneness Temple is completed, sometime in 2006, an entirely new level of experience will become possible, not only for those newly undergoing the twenty-one-day process, but also for the deeksha phenomenon worldwide.

I was relaxed in bed, just about to fall asleep, when the phone rang. It was Kiara calling from Europe; he had just finished his second public talk about the deekshas and Bhagavan's enlightenment process. When I hung up the phone, waves and waves of energy enveloped me. It was one of the most beautiful experiences I had ever had, and it had been initiated just from the energy of his voice over the phone!

Kiara, Grace, and I have been close friends for many years, and Kiara had e-mailed me about the experiences that he and Grace had in India with Bhagavan and Amma. Until that moment, I had been skeptical.

A couple of months later, Grace was in the San Francisco Bay Area, giving her first deekshas in the United States. Although I was really curious, I did not feel drawn to drive the five hours it would take to meet with her.

Shortly afterward, I was sitting outside in the sun, reading the manuscript of Kiara's book. Suddenly, the energy of the book entered my heart. A vortex of energy spun out of my heart and pulled me up out of my chair. The next thing I knew, I was on the phone asking Grace when she was giving her next deeksha. I packed my bags and hopped into the car.

Grace had a beautiful, sacred space for her deeksha gathering. One of my personalities was so, so eager to have some big experience of enlightenment with fireworks and cosmic consciousness. I expected something very extraordinary, beyond all my previous experiences. Even though most parts of me knew better, that expectation was still there.

At the end of the evening, I told Grace that I didn't think I felt anything from the deeksha, thanked her, and left. It's funny how I had forgotten the quiet space I went into and the rush of energy that came into my crown and out my hands.

That night, I didn't sleep. Instead, I had interdimensional experiences. There was a lot of emotional release of issues of which I had been totally unaware. At one point, a thick flip book was shown to me. As each page flipped by, I knew that that issue was gone forever. The pictures flipped by so rapidly that I couldn't even see or feel them all, and it didn't matter. I was amazed. *Could it be that simple?*

Next in this deep state that night, I found myself tearing up pages and pages of old plans and contracts for this life. My life was being totally rewritten! With this, there was a feeling of excitement. Part of me said, "Uh-oh. Watch out. You are in for *big* changes!"

I began hosting deeksha gatherings and getting deekshas from many people. During one deeksha, as Bhagavan's sandals were placed on my head, a golden ball entered my crown, dropped to my heart, and filled my being. I had a sense that all there is, is Bhagavan or God and that nothing "I" do matters. There is nothing for "me" to do. All is the Divine working through "me." I had known this before in principle, but this took me much, much further.

Occasionally, I would go into states of heightened awareness and profound stillness, experiencing a peace that permeated even my physical body so that it couldn't move. This peace and stillness must have transformed my nervous system, for one day, I became aware that stress and fear were no longer a possibility for me. The stillness and all-pervading silence became stronger and were always present.

These experiences, and others, were so beautiful. At the same time, the ugliness of the mind became more apparent. My smallest criticisms and judgments felt so very ugly and painful because of the sense of separation that they caused. I was helpless to free myself from them, and at the same time knew that there would be freedom from them at some point.

So much was changing so rapidly. I hadn't even gone to India for any courses, nor did I want to. In sharing my experiences with a friend, she reminded me of a vision and dream that I have had repeatedly for about fourteen years, showing me my life's work or purpose. *Of course!* Giving deekshas was what I had been shown in the visions and dreams, so I arranged to go to the twenty-one-day course in India that would be held in Golden City.

I knew that my process in the twenty-one-day course would be still, solid, peaceful, grounded, and very strong. However, there was a part of me expecting and wanting a powerful, "knock your socks off" experience with fireworks. Yes, I wanted the one hundred thousand orgasms that Freddy had talked about. Even though in my core I knew that "I" was not in charge, I had built up quite a few concepts and expectations about the entire adventure.

One of the first things we did in the opening of the twenty-one-day course was to prostrate and surrender to the Divine in whatever form or formlessness of Spirit that was appropriate for each individual. I was beginning to become more and more acutely aware of the many parts of what I call "me," and a part of me spoke up. She said, "Well, I'm not too much into this prostration thing, but I'll give it a try. And I'll surrender 100 percent."

As my forehead touched the floor, I heard a loud voice from inside—yet outside—myself speaking. "There is no surrendering to be done. The commitment was made long ago. There is nothing to do." I found myself sobbing in gratitude.

One of the most beautiful souls I've ever met, Anandagiri, spoke to us about our program and how it would be different from previous courses. One of the changes was that we would not be receiving hands-on deekshas. We would be spending time almost every day with beings who are in a very high state of union with the Divine: cosmic beings. The energy radiating from them would serve to transform us.

During the previous year, my mind chatter frequently had slowed almost to a halt. The silence often pervaded, but by that evening a definite personality began to arise in me who was chattering up a storm. She was quite a whiner and complainer. Her dialogue went something like this: "What, no deekshas? I came all the way to India and there are no deekshas! It's too hot here. I spent a lot of money getting here. Nothing is going on. I want to just go home." Her voice became louder and louder, especially as the fire began to rise in my body from the energy and the temperature outside. At times, the dialogue would take over the mind, and it would run in circles nonstop. It seemed out of character for me. What was going on? It was as though I had a new personality, and I wasn't very pleased with it.

The next several days of the course were about clearing family relationships, childhood issues, and birth issues. I had done lots of work on myself before, and all that seemed complete.

So I just sat there. Suddenly, I was flooded with light pouring down over and through me. I was going through some sort of rebirth. I began to laugh as I realized a small mistaken concept I had formulated during the process of birth. It was as if there were instructions for life on planet earth, and I had read them incorrectly. I thought that I had come here "to be loved" when the true instruction for life is "to love." My heart felt as though it had burst open, and tears flowed from the corners of my eyes.

The gifts of connection to the Divine and exquisite inner experiences continued. Throughout the weeks, we continued to sit almost daily with the cosmic beings. On the inner level, I heard one of them say that I was one of them. Our guides continued to lead us beautifully, step by step along the path. I experienced myself as the Buddha, and merged with Gayatri and other divine beings. There was an experience of the golden ball coming into my third eye and dropping to my heart, followed by my heart opening and the light flooding out. Then, a procession of beings lined up to enter my heart. I recalled the shift in consciousness for which we went, ages ago, to Egypt; and I recalled being with Bhagavan before.

So many exquisite gifts were given, and still that new personality went on and on, "Nothing is going on. It's too hot. Why don't they fix the air conditioner? I might as well go home! Blah, blah, blah." This personality seemed so unrelated to what I usually experienced as "me." "She" was screaming as if her life depended on it, and, in a way, it did.

Bhagavan has said, "You are not responsible for what you are." My guide said that who we think we are arises from our genetics, our birth, our childhood, our life experiences, mass consciousness, the atmosphere, and the temperature. I felt that she said the part about the temperature directly to me. The extreme heat from the weather and the energy pulsing through me had set this whining personality in motion.

When Bhagavan had a school, there were signs posted with his teachings. One of them read, "Your body is not your body. Your thoughts are not your thoughts. The self is only a concept."

I had full understanding and awareness of the first principle, "Your body is not your body." In 1989, I had been praying for an experience to show me that I was more than the body. One night, I was thrown from a moving car and experienced death. I was looking down on the body and was given a choice to come back into the injured body or to be born as a baby. I was in such ecstasy from the death experience that it didn't matter too much which I chose. In a way, it was like shopping for a new coat. Which one did I want to wear? I chose the adult, injured body.

A few years later, I began to have experiences showing me the truth of the teaching, "Your thoughts are not your thoughts." My mind would become still, and I could actually see thoughts form as shapes rolling right up to my mind. Then, they would be perceived as my thoughts if my mind engaged them.

But I had not had direct experience of the principle, "The self is only a concept." I knew it, but I knew it as a concept, not an experience. I also did not realize how much my idea of myself was intertwined with all the personalities that arose in me. I was so identified with my more familiar personalities. I might not have had the following experience, had not the complaining personality arisen in me during this course.

Our guide told a story about a devotee of Bhagavan. He had asked Bhagavan for enlightenment. Bhagavan paused and replied, "Who wants enlightenment?" The devotee turned and looked behind himself. He saw all his personalities, or "selves," behind him.

As I heard this, I looked behind me and saw all the personalities who I thought were "me" lined up behind me. When my awareness came into the space of the body, there was no thing, nothing there.

That which I called me was just the unlimited vastness. There were no boundaries. Thoughts, the sense of a body, personalities, relationships, and universes would arise and drop away like clouds passing across the sky. Behind it all, as the background, was just the limitless vastness. There was only stillness and peace. That is the truth of who I am, who you are, and who we all are.

I felt so much gratitude, and I knew that this would be a permanent transformation. There was nowhere to go; there was no state to reach. The search was over.

The next day, we went to Amma's abode, some miles away. The energy for her darshan felt very high and electric. Toward the end, she asked for our prayers so she could give us what we wanted. During the first few days of the course, I had experienced the suffering of humanity very painfully, on individual and global levels. The prayer that I heard pour forth from me was to please let me humbly and quietly play a very large role in the evolution of humanity as we all move into oneness. Tears flowed down my face as I prayed.

In the front rows of Amma's abode, people were seated who had been empowered to give deekshas. Amma then sent a wave of energy to them to give deekshas. At that moment, the wave of energy hit me, opening up a very wide and clear area of silence and energy in my head and above my head for six to seven feet. Above that, it narrowed and extended farther than I could sense. This has remained permanently open. I have no other words to describe this, nor do I have words for the depth of my gratitude.

Now, at home two weeks after the twenty-one-day course, the journey continues. The silence grows ever more profound, the intuition is stronger, and I wake in the morning with my heart so full of love that it brings tears to my eyes. It seems that there is no greater joy than this stillness and love. I know that this is just the beginning. Yet there is no beginning and no ending. There is only this present moment.

18.

Minanda

Minanda Fritz (minanda@livshalsa.se) has a degree in
Cognitive Psychotherapy and is a practicing psychologist and
a yoga teacher from Sweden. Minanda and her husband,
Parlan Fritz, were two of the organizers of the Experience
Festival, where I was first introduced to Bhagavan's work.
Parlan is also the coordinator for various Oneness Festivals
currently being organized around the world (see also www.
globaloneness.com, a comprehensive spiritual web site, featur-
ing thousands of articles in various categories). Grace and I
have become good friends of Minanda and Parlan.

I have noticed that different people have different kinds of
mystical experiences. Some, like Minanda, are clairvoyant, and
their experiences tend to be visual. Others tend to be clairau-
dient or kinesthetic, and their experiences tend to be auditory
or physical. Some people are none of these, but have a strong
sense of intuitive knowing. Some have several or all of these
pathways acutely developed. Others may have none of these
pathways developed, yet the work of transformation could still
be going on below the surface of their conscious awareness. It
is important to realize that enlightenment may or may not be
associated with mystical experiences. It is not so important
what realities we are able to perceive: it is our ability to embrace
the circumstances of our lives and to be used as vehicles for the
Divine that matters.

⁓

I have always been open and sensitive to energies, and I have had a few mystical experiences in my life.

I have known about Amma and Bhagavan for about five years. I have also attended many courses and spent quite a lot of time in Golden City. When my husband and I arrived in Golden City in August 2005, we heard about a new kind of darshan that piqued our curiosity.

This darshan centered on cosmic beings. Apparently, some of the guides had moved into profound states of enlightenment, and the darshan was to sit with these cosmic beings and meditate.

I was fortunate to be able to attend these darshans almost daily for twenty days. I have never in my life had such mystical and transformative experiences. I am sharing some of these experiences as accurately as possible, although it is difficult to translate them into written language.

Everyone seems to have a very personal experience when they attend the cosmic beings darshan, and there is no right or wrong experience. My belief is that those who are not aware of the energy transfer and activation that takes place during the darshans benefit from it anyway.

The first time that I attended the darshan in the hall where the cosmic beings were sitting, I didn't feel anything. There were seven guides sitting in chairs, and one empty chair. Later, I was told the empty chair was left empty because a well-known Indian yogi always came in during the darshans to sit in the chair.

As soon as I sat down and started meditating, I felt a strong connection, especially with two of them, one a female guide and the other a male guide. In my inner vision, I could feel the woman strongly radiating love and I saw light bubbles in the form of hearts coming from her heart. From the male guide, I saw waves coming from his knees and from beneath himself, strong waves of aqua light.

I spoke to them inwardly and asked for cosmic enlightenment. At first, nothing happened. Then, I added, "You are doing your dharma if you give me enlightenment; then, I can also do my dharma and share this with other people."

Suddenly, a huge bubble of light appeared, as big as the whole hall. It came down from the ceiling, and integrated itself within me. I experienced a sense of total emptiness. There was nothing and no one except this total emptiness, total presence. I found that I was so filled with light and energy that I could not walk for a long time afterward.

The experiences continued throughout the next few days. In one experience, I felt bubbles of light pouring down through my crown chakra. I could see that all of the cosmic beings were engulfed in an aqua light. Above each of them was a large eye, and above them all, there was one very large eye.

I received strong light from the cosmic beings. The whole air seemed to be filled with light bubbles. I found myself lifted inside a large bubble of light, and felt little bubbles being placed all over my body. Like an astronaut, I flew upward into the sky. Soon, I came to a dome made of white petals, which opened like a lotus. I fell into the dome of petals, spiraling down in complete darkness for quite a while. I was placed inside a coffin, symbolizing that "I" had to die. Then, suddenly, I found myself sitting inside a sun, radiating light. Again, I was so completely absorbed in light that my body felt very heavy, and it was difficult to walk afterward.

There were several times where I experienced a kind of dismemberment. I would feel golden hands moving around, massaging my brain or removing and replacing different parts of my body. Sometimes I felt something like wires being connected in the center of my brain, as though they were replacing the worn-out spark plugs in an engine.

One day, I felt a light blue brain with wings arriving from the right, and the golden hands placed the new brain into my skull. I asked for enlightenment. Again, a big light bubble appeared above my head and integrated itself into my whole body. I was lifted up to the ceiling and saw the whole hall from above. Then, I was inside a transparent golden bubble, traveling swiftly.

I traveled for long time to the sun, arriving inside the sun. In the center of the sun, Mother Mary slowly appeared as a light being. She stood in front of me. Mother Mary took my hands, put them together in front of my heart, and did something with my hands. First, she was reading from some sort of book. Then, she was blowing wind on the book and toward me, and the letters in the book became stardust. This stardust entered my eyes and my head, upon which my head turned into light. My hands were shaking uncontrollably.

After that, another large light being, maybe three times taller than a human being, appeared in front of me. It was Christ. He placed his hands on top of my head and gave me a deeksha. My whole body became light. I was so infused with light that I was unable to move my body at all for a couple of hours.

At the next darshan, I got a strong connection with the being in the empty chair. I was praying my usual prayer for grace when suddenly a being approached me from the empty chair. He was a beautiful young man, around sixteen years old, with black hair tied in the back. After a while, the young man changed into a very old and small yogi. He placed his hands on my heart and my head, and gave me energy until I had totally absorbed it and was feeling high on the light.

He took me through what seemed to be a shamanic reorganization of my physical body. He removed my eyes and put in new eyes. He opened my neck and removed long strings of what looked to be black weeds. He went through my entire body, cleaning out these black weeds. After that, immense light came into my body. He then went back to his chair. He muttered, "Now, you've gotten what you wanted" and then disappeared. He came several times afterward, checking the electricity in the spine, rewiring the electrical circuits, and balancing the energy in the body.

I had other experiences. For example, one day, I met Krishna. And another day, I rode on a white horse with Bhagavan.

My experiences with the cosmic beings seem to have permanently opened up my perceptions. After my stay in Golden City, we went to visit the ashram of Sri Aurobindo and the Mother in Pondicherry. I had strong experiences with them, where they both appeared to my inner vision, welcomed me, and showed me things. I had not seen them before, but afterward, when I saw pictures of the Mother, I realized it was she I had seen in my vision, except that she had appeared younger.

After this experience at Sri Aurobindo and the Mother's ashram in Pondicherry, I realized that something had changed during my stay in Golden City. What I before could sense as a powerful energy now regularly happens as a mystical experience. I can only say that grace has opened me up to experience more realities; and for that, I am so grateful!

When I now give deekshas, I feel that Amma and Bhagavan are very much present. I feel that they are so close to me, and their grace is flowing through me more than ever.

Empty Vessel

Was there ever a longing
That was empty of truth?
Is the bee ever drawn
To a nectarless flower?
Then, why bang my head on walls?
I have identified with the "seeker"
When all that I am
Is a vessel to be emptied!
I am so full of myself,
Pictures, expectations, longings—
What happens if I surrender it all?
True surrender is an act of grace,
Surrendering even the need to surrender.
In letting go, I am already filled.
In giving up control,
Every dream I have ever had
Finds its home.
So hard, yet so easy,
It takes a million to realize
That it only takes an instant.
I've hit bottom in the bottomless pit of desire.
I am ready for you now, beloved Friend.

III

Collective Journey of Enlightenment

19.

Mukti Avatars

Who are these people, Bhagavan and Amma, who are having such an extraordinary impact upon the world? Were they born avatars? When did Bhagavan first become aware of his mission? And Amma of hers? How do they propose to enlighten the world? What are the limits of their capabilities?

I had often imagined what it would have been like to know an enlightened being such as Jesus personally: to walk with him, to witness his miracles, and to ask him these kinds of questions. Little did I know that I would one day be led to Golden City and witness a revolution in human consciousness perhaps unparalleled in human history!

Who is Bhagavan? The term means different things to different people. "Anyone in India can call himself a bhagavan," he says jokingly, "and there is no need for controversy around this."

He does acknowledge himself as an avatar, however. He says, "An avatar comes to earth in response to humanity's call. He comes when there is a certain level of stagnation, and he comes with a specialized mission. An avatar embodies the descent of higher consciousness. The person need not necessarily be a spiritual being. For instance, Gandhi was an avatar of nonviolence, and Einstein was an avatar of physics. Any higher consciousness taking birth can be called an avatar." He refers to himself as the avatar of enlightenment. His mission is to give enlightenment to the world.

Many consider Bhagavan to be a *poorna* avatar, a total embodiment of divinity. Throughout the ages, avatars have descended to kindle the forces of enlightenment in a few people, but Bhagavan's mission is to kindle a collective manifestation of divinity in the mass consciousness of the planet. I believe that Bhagavan does not represent an individual so much as collective consciousness, the same consciousness that is known variously as Christ consciousness, Buddha consciousness, or Unified consciousness.

Bhagavan was born on March 7, 1949, in a village in Tamil Nadu called Natham. He was given the name Vijay Kumar. Ever since he was two or three, he has been aware that he is a descent of divinity here on earth to serve humanity. He tells of how his parents would take him to the temple when he was young and circumambulate around the images of various gods and goddesses. All of a sudden, he would find himself inside these images and have to stop moving. People would ask him why he was not moving, and he would say, "I am inside this deity looking out. How can I move myself around?"

He did not experience suffering and was always in a very happy state. At first, he thought that everybody was like him, but when he saw that they were suffering, he realized that his job was to bring them out of suffering. This knowing was within him already at the age of four or five.

One of the games played by the village children was enacting the ancient stories. He was always chosen to play Krishna or one of the gods, and would be asked for various boons, and they were always granted. Even the elders of the village would come up to him and put some grains in his hand; he would bless the grain and they would have good crops.

At age nine or so, the golden ball began to appear to him. He realized it could be sent into people in order to help them awaken, but he was not able to activate it at first. After working with it for a long time, certain chants would come to him, and as he chanted these words, it would become activated. He continued working with this golden ball through adulthood, experimenting in many ways to see how it could be used to help people.

When he was twenty-eight or so, some mutual friends introduced him to his future wife, Padmavati, now known as Amma. She was born on August 15, 1954, in a village called Sangam. She was a mystic and would go into states of samadhi from early childhood. She, too, was deeply concerned for humanity, and felt that she was here to liberate people from suffering. From the time she was little, she let her parents and childhood friends know that she would marry only God, and would know him when she saw him. Strange as they thought this was, they accepted this.

When they were introduced to each other, they immediately recognized each other and knew that they were meant to be together and work together. She had first seen him in a statue in a temple, and knew that soon she would be meeting him. Her childhood dream was fulfilled. Their marriage took place on June 9, 1976.

Amma had already become quite well known for her mystical powers, and her ability to grant boons and perform miracles. She was regarded in her village as an aspect of the Divine Mother. When she left her village, the entire village became sad: A divine power had left.

There is a story that when some villagers first saw her picture taken along with Bhagavan they became furious. How dare this man sit beside her! They eventually reconciled themselves to the idea that because she had said that she would marry God, this must be God. So that was how it began for many of the villagers!

There was a time when Bhagavan was the director of a school in Andhra Pradesh known as Jeevashram. He realized that many social ills stemmed from a faulty educational system, and was interested in helping to create a new model of education that concerned itself with the flowering of the heart as well as the intellect.

It was during this time that the miracle of enlightenment first happened. Bhagavan had always known that he was able to help people in various ways—grant them boons, heal their illnesses, and so on—but he wasn't able to liberate them yet. One day, his son, Krishna, came bounding into the classroom very excitedly saying that a golden ball had entered into him, and was causing him to experience all kinds of wonderful states of consciousness.

"All right," said Bhagavan very composedly. "See if you can pass it on to someone else." So the boy passed it on to a classmate, and she had the same experience of being able to enter into cosmic consciousness and experience other *lokas,* or dimensions. Of course, it was all being done by Bhagavan. In this way, many students from this school received divine experiences, and subsequently chose to help Bhagavan in his mission. Many of these former students are now disciples and active members of Oneness University.

This was back in 1989, and was the beginning of Bhagavan's experiments with giving enlightenment to people. The passing on of enlightenment spread like wildfire. As students began experiencing these enlightened states, all kinds of strange things started happening. They could make the winds start and stop, they could make the rains come and go, they could enter into other times and lokas, they could enter in and out of pictures, and they could heal people with a touch. Not only that, people simply walking or driving on the road outside Jeevashram were also beginning to spontaneously experience all kinds of mystical phenomena.

But soon the parents began to get upset. "What is happening to my child?" they asked. Bhagavan realized that he would have to take it slower, and he withdrew these powers. Eventually, at the repeated requests of his students, he agreed to create an order of disciples, with the only requirement being that they joined with their parents' permission and blessing.

This order of disciples has grown throughout the years and now numbers about 180 member-guides. During the first few years of the order, Bhagavan was still not very sure about giving enlightenment to the masses. This shifted in the middle of 2003. Up until that time, he did not know for certain whether this grand experiment of global enlightenment would succeed in time to avert global catastrophe. After this point, it felt as though something had shifted, and he knew with absolute certainty then that his mission would succeed, and that humanity would make it. We were divinely destined to move into the Golden Age, and mass enlightenment could now take place.

With the first guides, the deeksha was given directly by Bhagavan himself. The work was still very experimental, and the results were not always predictable. Some of these first guides went into nonfunctional states of *nirvikalpa* samadhi for months. It was a blissful divine state, but not very useful as far as actively working in the world.

Gradually, he was able to modify the deeksha so that a person could experience high states of samadhi and still remain functional in the world. As he continued experimenting with the transfer of power coming through him and acting upon the neurobiological circuits in the brain to create the conditions for enlightenment, he realized at a certain point that anyone, and everyone, was capable of becoming enlightened.

It was only after this realization that he began his work with the masses; he had hesitated earlier because he didn't want anybody to feel left out.

Many of the first guides had been experiencing cosmic states of consciousness throughout the years that he had been working with them. Few of them, however, had attained the permanent state of enlightenment. In June 2003, Bhagavan called them together, and had them go through forty-two days of intense *sadhana,* during which he personally gave them deeksha. Each of them became permanently enlightened.

As the work proceeded, the power of the deeksha grew. In the early stages, he would have people go through eighteen months on a fruit-only diet to heighten the sensitivity of their subtle bodies. This is no longer necessary now. He found that what was taking eighteen months to prepare for soon took two months, and then three weeks, and then ten days. He began training the enlightened guides to do the deekshas themselves. As they attuned to his consciousness, and transferred the golden ball to others, he was able to follow the energy of the deekshas and do the necessary work "divine of surgery." In later phases, he found that he was able to do this entirely from a distance.

It was after this that the floodgates of enlightenment began to open. He began to give deeksha to larger groups of people, both Indian and Western. The first public deekshas for enlightenment were given on the occasion of Amma's birthday, on August 17, 2003. A few days later, the first week-long deeksha course was given for Westerners. Grace and I were among this group.

At this same time, he also started giving deeksha to masses of Indian devotees, including entire villages. Many hundreds began coming every day from throughout the country for one-

day programs—a short teaching followed by a deeksha—
which has now been extended to three-day programs.

In early 2004, longer courses started being offered to
laypeople from all over the world. Several ten-day courses were
offered, along with even more profound twenty-one-day
courses designed to take people into the state of oneness
deeply enough that they themselves could transfer the deeksha
of enlightenment to others. Many people worldwide are now
prepared to give deeksha. A continually updated list of deeksha givers can be found on the web sites listed in the back of
this book.

The next stage of Bhagavan's program for mass enlightenment is the completion of the Oneness Temple being built in
Golden City. The design of this temple uses a form of ancient
Vedic sacred geometry known as *vaasthu,* and will serve as a
physical anchor for the next stage of Bhagavan's work. Sacred
geometrical proportions used in the Mayan and Egyptian pyr-
amids have also been incorporated into the design.

The plan is to have as many as eight thousand enlightened people meditating in it at any given time, creating a
strong morphogenetic field of enlightenment and transmitting this state directly into the mass consciousness of
humanity. It will be completed toward the end of 2006. It is
expected that once this is completed, Bhagavan's ability to
transfer states of enlightenment to the masses will increase
exponentially. People will simply have to walk through this
field in order to experience a witness state, which is the first
stage of enlightenment.

As the power of the deeksha grows around the world
through the increasing numbers of people who are being
trained as deeksha givers, Bhagavan emphasizes that the deeksha should be adapted to the local culture and religion. There

is nothing intrinsically Hindu about enlightenment. If he had been born in China, he says, the same work would have a Taoist flavor; if he had been born in the West, it would have a Christian flavor; if he had been born in the Middle East, it would have a Muslim or Jewish flavor; and for a growing minority of people around the world who consider themselves outside any religious boxes, it would have a metaphysical or universal flavor.

We need to be extremely sensitive that as the work proceeds in different parts of the world, or even in India, that it not become a religion or a cult. From the perspective of cosmic union, it makes no difference whether the gift of enlightenment comes through Bhagavan or Christ or White Buffalo Woman or Allah or Krishna or Inanna or Buddha or whatever image of the Deity or wholeness one believes in.

"You can have a picture of Jesus on the altar and give the deeksha, and the results will be the same," he emphasizes. Organized religions, when used to divide people, usually cause more harm than good, and the last thing he wants to do is to create yet another religion. Once our guiding light comes from within, Bhagavan predicts all religions will, die a natural death.

Bhagavan expects that once the critical mass of people is achieved, it will only be a matter of a few months before the rest of humanity becomes sensitive to the increasingly strong morphogenetic fields of the enlightened state. There will be a moment when a doorway between the worlds opens, and humanity will step through this doorway collectively as an enlightened species.

Bhagavan is manifesting, I am told, only a tiny fraction of his power at this time. He could turn up the volume any time he chooses, but it needs to proceed in stages. He recognizes that to unleash too much *shakti* at once could be painful and destructive, so he is holding himself back. As the work grows, and the morphogenetic field of enlightenment gets stronger, more and more of his power will be revealed, until all structures of human separation collapse in the face of this rising tide.

It is expected that as the strength of these morphogenetic fields continues to grow, more and more people will begin to move into a permanent state of enlightenment with just a single deeksha. Soon, it will become possible for anyone who has received deeksha to give deeksha to anyone else and give them enlightenment as well. Eventually, even the individual deeksha will not be required.

The state will be transferred through a glance, through a touch, or through a prayer. It will happen through dance, music, and art. It will happen as people in the healing professions go about their daily work. It will happen as people fall in love. It will happen as people open their hearts and eyes to suffering humanity. It will happen spontaneously as an unstoppable tide of grace coursing through our collective consciousness.

Already, spontaneous awakenings are beginning to happen all over the world. Perhaps the morphogenetic fields are already strong enough for those whose souls are ready. It is a feedback loop. The greater the number of people who become enlightened, the stronger the morphogenetic fields of enlightenment will become. This, in turn, will cause the DNA of the human species to mutate in a positive way, which will then modify our nervous systems to naturally receive enlightenment.

In the years to come, spiritual seeking may become unnecessary, even counterproductive. A state of relaxed openness may be more effective, as we open ourselves to an evolutionary force that is so much bigger than anything we know. What is coming is unimaginable and will not fit into our spiritual and intellectual boxes. All teachings and practices will become irrelevant as the power of this wave sweeps through our collective being.

Bhagavan is clear that this is the age of the collective avatar. The new cosmic creation emerging in our midst is too vast to be manifested through a single embodiment. He is a major point of descent for the Supreme One, but ultimately, it will descend everywhere, through everyone. His mission is to prepare the way, so that all of us together, as a group avataric force, become the architects of a new cosmic cycle. Once this happens, he says, his own work will be done

This is not a passive event, but a cocreative act. As we become collectively enlightened, we become this avataric force. It will be an order of enlightenment far beyond anything we are now able to experience as separate enlightened individuals. The human family will begin to experience itself as one global entity, one rainbow of many colors, one planetary self with many pairs of eyes, one planetary brain composed of six billion central nervous systems!

What this will look like in the years and decades to come is beyond our wildest imaginings. This will be the new dawn so many have awaited in every age and tradition. This will be the day when the gates of eternity will be opened to all, and God's dream will be realized. Or perhaps it does not yet exist even in the mind of God, and is being dreamed into existence, cocreatively, moment by moment. This is why Bhagavan has taken incarnation. This is why we have taken incarnation. These are truly the times that we were born for!

A New Dawn

First streaks of dawn,
The twinkling lights of an age gone by
Fade into eternity past.
I wake up shivering
From my illusions of sleep.
Why must darkness precede the dawn?
Why is death the prelude to birth?
No matter:
The long night is ended now.
The first rays of a new dawn
Illuminate my path,
Beckoning me to follow.
Can I shape the coming day?

20.

Summary of Teachings

Having shared something about the journey itself, and the global mission that Amma and Bhagavan are here to accomplish, it is time to highlight some of Bhagavan's teachings.

First of all, what is enlightenment? Bhagavan defines it differently in different contexts. For a neurologist, it is the shutting down of certain parts of the parietal lobe. For a biologist, it is a heightening of the senses. For a psychologist, it is loss of the ego. For a philosopher, it is becoming a witness to life. For someone on a spiritual path, it is opening your heart to life, developing the capacity to love.

When asked to define *love,* Bhagavan says that he can only tell you what love is not. It is not about possessing another person. It is not rooted in neediness or attachment or fear of loss. It is not a justification to control somebody's life. What most people call love, he emphasizes, is not love. To experience the same love that Buddha or Christ felt, you require a mutation in your physical brain. Only then can you experience this level of love. No amount of spiritual or psychological effort can take you there.

To be enlightened, he stresses, is to be free from the sense of separate existence. The sense of a fixed identity disappears. Once you become enlightened, what exists is only the other. You experience oneness with all creation, and eventually oneness with God. You experience the gift of being human. You experience what it means to give and receive love.

In the realization of this oneness, there is joy. As long as the self exists, it can experience pleasure, but not joy. When things are going your way, you experience pleasure; when things are not, you experience pain. But this is very different from the "causeless" joy of pure being, in which you are no longer separate from any aspect of creation or Creator, no matter what the circumstances of your life.

Bhagavan says that the next best thing to enlightenment is knowing that you are not enlightened. This is not a frivolous statement. "Don't pretend to be enlightened if you are not," he cautions. The person on a spiritual path may have built up a spiritual persona around himself or herself that is as difficult to break through as any of the darker expressions of the mind—perhaps more so.

The main obstacle to enlightenment is not in the particular quality of the self-identity that we create, whether it is coarse or refined, material or spiritual, but in our degree of attachment to that identity. We spiritual people often assume that our journey toward enlightenment is a linear progression, and that we can become better and better people until someday we cross the finish line—and we're there.

It is perhaps easier for a spiritually unsophisticated person to get enlightened than someone who has walked a spiritual path for years and has many concepts and expectations about what enlightenment is or should be, or what she or he is or should be. Ironically, the more attached a person is to a spiritual persona, the more that person develops a spiritual ego, and the further she or he gets from the enlightened state. The mind delights in creating an "as if" image of the enlightened self. Now, it can continue its game of comparison and judgment, except on a more sophisticated level.

Being good does not threaten the survival of the mind, as long as we are simultaneously disowning the bad; being spiritual is fine as long as we continue judging ourselves or others for not meeting our expectations. We take the radiance of our divinity, which manages to shine dimly through the thick layers of the mind, and enshrine it with religiosity, stifle it with morality, distort it with self-righteousness, and objectify it with spiritual egoism.

I am not implying that it isn't desirable to strive to be moral, good, and loving. There is a reason that religions exist, and many people have found that the spiritual or psychological path refines or even transforms the ego. As a spiritual teacher and psychotherapist, I have seen the power of meditation, and of techniques such as Holotropic Breathwork, psychosynthesis, regression therapies, and bodywork, to help heal the traumas of the past and polish the rough edges of the personality.

If refining and clearing the mind is our quest, then by all means we must continue doing everything that we can in this direction. However, if enlightenment is our quest, we cannot get there by trying to develop enlightened qualities. We need to come to an understanding of the very nature of the mind.

In the courses offered at Oneness University, the first few days are about becoming aware of the prison of the mind. It isn't about trying to change any of it, because you cannot. You are simply witnessing the reality of your mind as it is, the emotional charge, the habit patterns, the assumptions, the traumas, the conditioning, and the masks that you have constructed in order to survive. As you witness, you begin to strip down the social and spiritual personas, and you begin to understand the nature of mind. You become aware that enlightenment is simply about disengaging from the mind.

Enlightenment is not a matter of changing the contents of the mind or getting rid of the mind. Enlightenment is recognizing the mind for what it is; then, it no longer has the power to make your decisions for you. It is not about becoming mindless, but rather about becoming what the Buddhists call mindful: being present with reality as it is.

Most of us identify with the mind, and this is why we suffer, for we are *not* the mind. The mind, however, can be a useful tool. After enlightenment, you find that you are no longer controlled by the mind, and can disengage from it when it is not needed. When the mind is needed, however, consciousness comes through and uses the mind with a sharpness, clarity, and versatility not possible before.

To disengage from the mind is to lose a sense of self as a fixed, separate, and continuous entity. Enlightenment is the realization that there is no self to get enlightened. We cannot change the nature of the mind. The mind is simply the mind, but after enlightenment, our relationship with the mind changes. We are no longer enslaved by the contents or conditioning of the mind. Thoughts may still come and go, emotions may still come and go, but we recognize that they are not "our" thoughts or emotions. With this recognition, we experience freedom.

Bhagavan teaches that there is no such thing as a personal mind. Yes, we have individual thoughts, but they are simply emanations from what he calls the ancient mind, a collective "thought sphere" of humanity that has existed from the beginnings of our current human civilization, perhaps eleven thousand or twelve thousand years. All our fears, inadequacies, turmoil, and pain; all our lusts, addictions, insecurities, and greed; and all our hatred, rage, jealousies, and judgments belong to this thought sphere. Additionally, many of our impulses for kindness, beauty, pleasure, happiness, and courage also exist within this thought sphere.

The brain is like a radio that picks up these frequencies according to our state of mind or health, physical environment, or various astrological factors. Our own individual traumas or conditioning from the past also contribute to our unconscious selection of which radio station to play.

However, our thoughts are not our own thoughts. Because the brain is programmed for separation, we receive these thoughts, feelings, impressions, and emotions as if they were our own, thereby allowing us to feel separate from the rest of humanity, which we perceive to be better than, less than, or somehow different from us.

We watch a movie on the screen and get lost in the illusion that it is real. However, if we slow it down so that we can see it frame by frame, we realize that it is only a movie. In the same manner, we are conditioned by the self to perceive our own life as a living movie.

Enlightenment fine-tunes the senses so that we realize that the impression of a fixed, continuous self is an illusion generated by the neurological circuitry of the brain. There is a continuous dance of personalities, but no fixed or continuous self that somehow remains the same from birth to death. Consciousness flows through the body moment by moment, but it is the same consciousness that flows through all creation.

When there is no self, there is no craving or attachment. Cravings and attachments are based on a sense of separate existence, or self-importance. When we crave or are attached, we continually desire things that we do not have, or have what we do not desire. When there is no separate self, attachments and cravings cease. When cravings and attachments cease, there is no suffering. We are not talking about physical or psychological suffering here, but existential suffering. Existential suffering is the incessant desire to be experiencing something other than what is. It is not pain that causes suffering, but resistance to that pain. It is our attempts to escape from suffering that cause us suffering!

Enlightenment means to experience the reality of each

moment as it comes your way, without needing to resist it or change it in any way. Once you are willing to fully experience what is here, you are no longer separate from reality. You experience the truth of each moment directly as it is. You become freed from the interference and conditioning imposed by the mind. You experience the causeless joy of being!

You still have mental pathways of old habits, memories, and personality, but you are no longer a solid thing. The self becomes porous, and the winds of eternity blow through freshly in every moment. You are no longer a fixed person, but a dance of personalities weaving in and out of awareness. You are not even a witness separate from yourself, watching things blowing in the wind. You are the wind.

You may still have likes and dislikes, and emotions may still come up, but there is no charge left; and no sooner do they come up than they go away, in the same way that an infant throws a tantrum one moment, and stares in wonderment at a caterpillar the next. There may still be emotional habit patterns imprinted in the body, but these, too, subside in time.

Another realization that comes after enlightenment is that your body is not your body. Most of the functions of the body are involuntary, but you realize that even the functions that you thought were voluntary are not really yours to control. Many people report that during an enlightenment experience, the body moves, cries, and laughs, completely independent of personal will. Or it may become immobile, and you realize that there is nothing that you can do to make it move, unless it chooses to.

Your relationship with your body changes. You no longer identify it as yours: Rather, it is a beautiful vehicle for consciousness to use. You understand how privileged you are to have this lovely, living body as a means to express the Divine in the world. Each taste, each smell, each sound, each vision, and each touch is exquisite, and is as if you were experiencing it for the first time. Each thought, likewise, comes with its own living freshness directly from the consciousness of each moment, an experience that the Zen Buddhists refer to as beginner's mind.

Enlightenment begins with the ability to witness all these things. As you move into more profound states of unity and God realization, you discover that you have become one with all creation, and that, indeed, the sense of your own body embraces all of creation. Eventually, you discover that you have become one with the Creator, as well as creation. You realize, in the words of Jesus two thousand years ago, that "I and the Father are One."

In a nutshell, Bhagavan teaches the following:

1. There is only one mind—the ancient mind. It is conditioned by separation and duality.

2. *Your mind is not your own mind,* but an extension of this ancient mind.

3. Similarly, *your thoughts are not your own thoughts,* but downloaded from the thought sphere associated with this ancient mind.

4. The sense of a separate self is generated by the neurobiological structure of the human brain.

5. This "self," in experiencing itself as separate, generates cravings, aversions, comparisons, and judgments, which are the cause of suffering.

6. When the self disappears, suffering ends. When cravings drop away, including the craving for enlightenment, you are enlightened.

7. When the deeksha is given, a neurobiological process begins, which leads to the dissolution of the sense of a separate, fixed self.

8. When the fixed self disappears, you experience yourself as simply a dance of personalities continually arising and passing away in a sea of consciousness. Underneath all these forms and personalities, you experience yourself as Atman, in oneness with all.

9. *Your body is not your body.* When the self disappears, your sense of ownership of the body disappears, and you experience it as a vehicle for the divine dance of consciousness. Eventually, all creation becomes your body.

10. The mind, based in duality, cannot be enlightened.

11. The self, which is an illusion, cannot be enlightened. *The self is only a concept.*

12. Enlightenment is the realization that there is no self to become enlightened. The seeker disappears in the realization of the absolute divine perfection of each moment!

21.

Deeksha and the Brain

Enlightenment is the ability to see reality as it is, without the layers of interference and interpretation imposed by the mind. It is a simple neurobiological event, and can happen in an instant. Paradoxically, in the moment of your enlightenment, you also discover that you have always been enlightened! It is our natural state!

The biocircuitry of a human being was designed in such a way that after developing a self at around age three, we would return naturally to a state of unified existence at around age eighteen. Unfortunately, something went awry, and we experienced a Fall as a species.

Nature demanded that there always be a select few throughout our subsequent history who maintained this morphogenetic field of the natural enlightened state. Historical figures such as the Buddha, Lao-tzu, Jesus, and many others exemplified this. Now, humanity is being prepared to return to our natural state as a species. The time has come for each of us to be restored to our natural enlightened state!

Enlightenment has nothing to do with how long you have been on a spiritual path or what your religious beliefs are. You do not even need to believe in God or have any concepts about the soul. Enlightenment does not depend on knowing the right teachings or mantras. It has nothing to do with how many lifetimes you have meditated, or even with how "good" a person you are.

There is nothing you can "do" to get enlightened. Enlightenment cannot be achieved through your own efforts any more than a drowning person can yank himself out of the water by his own hair. We are in a prison of the mind, and the key is on the other side. The mind cannot deactivate itself. *Enlightenment can happen only by grace.* It is part of a natural evolutionary impulse

Humanity is ready now, says Bhagavan. Each of us has spent lifetimes preparing for this. We have all done our sadhana, or whatever we thought was required, and it is time now to enter the Golden Age together. The question is not *if* we will get enlightened, but *when.*

"There is a simple way to know if you are enlightened," my guide had told me once. "If you are asking the question, you are not." And the biggest obstacle to enlightenment is to pretend that you already are if you are not.

If you know that you are not enlightened, and you become aware of the cravings and aversions generated by the illusion of self, then you become open to grace. When you see clearly the nature of the mind, and the extent of your conditioning, and when you become tired of the resulting suffering—all the incessant comparing, judging, striving, and blaming—then grace can begin to flow in. But understanding this as a concept isn't enough. It must be felt and experienced.

The means that Bhagavan has set up for this grace to act is known as the deeksha. The deeksha is a transfer of power, a type of initiation. It usually consists of a ceremony in which someone who has been initiated in the process places their hands upon your head in a state of divine union, and becomes a channel for this cosmic energy to reorganize your neurocircuitry.

Bhagavan refers to this process as divine surgery. A golden ball of divine grace descends through the crown chakra, and the kundalini channels get activated. Certain areas in the brain get shut down, and other areas get energized, initiating a process in which the entire brain and nervous system is reorganized.

This golden ball is programmed by Bhagavan to reorganize the biological circuitry of the brain, leading to enlightenment. It has a living intelligence, and operates differently within each person. Once it has descended into the crown chakra, the process will move toward completion, programmed by the divine *sankalpa*, or intent, of Amma and Bhagavan.

The deeksha punches through the wall of concepts set up by the mind. The winds of heaven can then blow through. As Carlos Castaneda teaches, when we move into the world of the *nagual*, our "assemblage point" shifts, and we are free.

Currently, the human brain is designed to serve as a radio that picks up a certain band of frequencies that are the ancient mind. The deeksha loosens up our attachment to these frequencies. It dissolves the feedback loops of consciousness that create the sense of separate identity, or self. The brain-radio is then able to pick up the much wider range of frequencies emanating from the Universal Mind.

To be enlightened is to access our souls directly, rather than through the interference of the mind. Unfortunately, for many people on the spiritual path, even though we have had direct experience of our souls from time to time, our concept of the soul is not very different from our concept of self. It is a higher self, but it is still perceived as a separate, fixed self. This concept can be a limitation, which is why Bhagavan doesn't speak much about the soul.

The enlightened yogis of ancient India, when they spoke of their inner divinity as the Atman, understood that there was no such thing as a fixed, individual soul. The individual is holographically related to the whole. The Atman is one with

Brahman, the universal field of consciousness that is constantly moving through each expression of creation. "*Tat twam asi,*" say the yogis. "I am That!"

What happens when the deeksha is given? Some immediately go into a peak experience of bliss, profound silence, or cosmic consciousness. This may or may not be permanent. If it isn't, this first peak experience is followed by other peak experiences in the course of time, until a permanent enlightened state establishes itself.

For others, there is no immediate felt response, and it may take hours, days, or weeks before they start noticing a change. Regardless, once the deeksha is received, the seed of enlightenment has been planted, and your divine self will work with you in accordance with it's own soul's purpose and the readiness of your physical body to bring the seed to fruition. Often, the first thing that comes up for people is an acute sensitivity to the nature of mind, and the patterns that have ruled their lives for so long. It can be a shocking and painful experience when we first begin to look at it, but it is necessary if we are to break free. If more than one deeksha is given, often the first deeksha is programmed to pinpoint the self-centeredness of the mind. If a person has done some self-examination and emotional clearing beforehand or has already "hit bottom," that can help. Grace flows only when you recognize your illusions. As long as you think that you can make it on your own, its flow will be impeded.

Once the deeksha is given, you cannot stop the process. Nor can you help it along, except by simply witnessing it. As Bhagavan asks, once the train pulls out from the station, will you get to your destination any faster by constantly running around back and forth inside the train? Enlightenment has nothing to do with the mind or the contents of the mind. It has everything to do with the brain, and the deeksha is an intelligent force that is programmed to do whatever is necessary to create the neurobiological shift necessary to get there!

So if a blocked personality shows up, simply step back and watch the way it works. There might be a fear that you will be the only person on earth who does not become enlightened, that you have too many mental blocks, that your heart isn't open enough, that you haven't done enough emotional clearing, that there is something wrong with you physically, that you are too old, too unworthy, too traumatized, or whatever your own personal story might be.

Just watch this personality as if you were watching a movie. Notice how attached it is to the drama of its own suffering. Notice how it sustains itself through its traumas and dramas, even the drama of planning its own enlightenment. Notice how it feeds itself by pretending to hate itself. Notice how its *idea* of being blocked *becomes* the block. Notice how it wants to analyze itself to death before it is ready to surrender. Notice how it hears only what it wants to hear, so it can forever prove itself right.

You may want to make a list of these escape routes of the mind. Give these "negative" personalities a voice, and describe in detail all their fears, doubts, blocks, manipulations, denials, and dysfunctional habit patterns that you can think of. Then, let it all go. Once it is down on paper, you may find that they no longer have as much power over you. Once you can see clearly, the seeing itself is the liberation. Once you realize that there is nothing that you can do to change yourself, then surrender can happen, and grace can flow.

For some people, even the act of surrender is associated with a great effort. Well, then, surrender even your effort to surrender. Simply ask for grace and then be silent. Once this "you" who is so intent on understanding, changing, or healing itself surrenders, enlightenment can happen easily. The neurological shift takes place, and you return to your natural state of oneness. It is as simple as that.

It is important to understand what enlightenment is not. It is not about losing your mind, or even changing the nature of your mind. The same mind continues to exist, although you notice that you now have a different relationship with it. Nor is enlightenment equated with cosmic bliss, instant clairvoyant abilities, or high spiritual states. All these may accompany or follow enlightenment at some point, but it is not what enlightenment is about. Enlightenment is simply "throwing a switch" in the neurobiological structures of your brain, and thereby dissolving the sense of a separate self. It is not about changing the contents of the mind, but seeing the mind for what it is. In this very seeing, all conflict and suffering dissolves, and you experience freedom.

Perhaps one indication that a person is enlightened is that she is no longer trying to become enlightened. In fact, she is not trying to become anything so much as experiencing the fullness of who she already is. Suffering is essentially the resistance to experiencing reality as it is. Once enlightened, you will no longer be forever seeking to change, deny, defend, or deify your experience of reality. You will naturally experience the present moment for what it is.

The difference is primarily internal. An enlightened person can still make mistakes, still experience disappointments, still have difficulty with relationships, still experience limitations, and still be bad-tempered; but he will no longer be identified with these characteristics. It is not required that an enlightened person always have a radiant aura or be cheerful.

In fact, there will be times when an enlightened person

will need to exhibit anger where she would normally be a doormat, or do something quite contrary to an established social or moral code because she is no longer bound by the conditioned identities and learned responses of the old order. An enlightened person discovers joy in being true to herself. She finds no need to pretend anymore, although to an unenlightened consciousness, she might well be perceived as a troublemaker!

To be enlightened is to peel off the layers of interpretation from a given event. To the enlightened person, life becomes a very ordinary thing. You walk, and you are walking. You eat, and you are eating. Enlightenment is not about having extraordinary experiences so much as recognizing that each ordinary moment is extraordinary in itself. Before, there were a thousand interpretations in the mind for everything you experienced. Now, there is only the experience.

There is a difference between enlightenment experiences and the state of enlightenment. Enlightenment experiences are peak experiences or high energy experiences. You may go into a peak experience after a deeksha. You may already have had several peak experiences through the course of your life. The kundalini energies within your body rise up to the top of the head, unite with the cosmic energies, and you experience bliss, unconditional love, or cosmic consciousness. You may see celestial visions or even journey into various lokas, or heavenly realms.

Peak experiences cannot be sustained beyond a few hours or, at most, a few days. The cosmic energies coursing through your nervous system would burn you out and short-circuit the human body, at least in our current level of human evolution. An enlightened state, on the other hand, is permanent. It is a shift in the neurobiological pathways of the brain, resulting in the sharpening of the senses, and the subsequent loss of a fixated self.

After a deeksha, there is often a sequence of one or more peak experiences, which will eventually stabilize into enlightenment as a permanent state.

This can be illustrated in the form of a graph. Supposing the unenlightened person operates from a −2, −3, or −4, depending on his level of suffering. When the deeksha is given, it will catapult him into a +3 or +4, where he may experience phenomena associated with unity consciousness. This peak experience will not last long; and after a few hours, the phenomena will subside. However, once he has experienced an enlightened state, he will generally not dip below the positive numbers. He may stabilize at +1 or +2. During the next deeksha, he may go up to +4 or +5, and then stabilize at +2 or +3. The stabilizing point is higher with each successive peak experience.

22.

Journey of Enlightenment

There is an assumption that once you are enlightened, you will never experience sadness, grief, anger, jealousy, or pain; that somehow you have overcome all negative thoughts or emotions. This is far from the truth. The nature of the mind is unchanged. The contents of the mind may also remain unchanged. But without the self to dictate terms, or to differentiate so obsessively between right and wrong, you experience that the "charge" begins to disappear. You become established in a state of witnessing. And enlightenment is a continuously deepening process.

Many people associate enlightenment with tremendous states of cosmic consciousness, clairvoyant perception, omniscience, and so on. All these may or may not be associated with the state, but should not be mistaken for enlightenment. Enlightenment itself is a very simple event, and is simply the dissolution of the sense of separateness. It is the natural state in which your body is designed to be.

To become enlightened is to be comfortable with the flow of life. If you are feeling sad, you are not trying to talk yourself out of it. If you are feeling happy, you are not trying to hold onto that feeling. Everything simply is what it is, without a carryover from past associations, traumas, or conditioned patterns intruding on the experience of the moment. You become fully present with each emotion and with each experience. You find, as the guides enjoy reminding people, that every emotion, when fully experienced, becomes bliss.

Each person's enlightenment is unique. Bhagavan says that if there are six billion people on Earth, there will be six billion kinds of enlightenment. Each person's enlightenment will incorporate qualities of their own soul's desires and purpose. As you progress, you may discover a natural gift for healing or a great capacity for wisdom or a profound caring for Earth and humanity. You may experience a deep inner silence or an all-pervading joy or a state of oneness with all creation. These states may come and go, and vary from person to person, but there is one thing that every enlightened person will experience: the end of suffering.

You will still have desires, but they won't turn into cravings. You will still have resistances, but they won't turn into aversions. You will still have a personality, but it will be a fluid dance of personalities that come and go. As you grow into the state, you will not feel the need to hold onto resentments, fears, or traumas, nor will you feel the need to hold onto good times or spiritual highs.

In your enlightened state, there will be continually more profound states of oneness, peace, stillness, love, and joy. You will find yourself more and more at home in the mystical realms, and also, paradoxically in the physical realms.

At first, however, the mind might throw up all kinds of conflict, resistance, and doubt. It is the nature of the self to resist change, and this has become a memory pattern within the mind. This may well come up with great force as the mind tries to deny the experience. Simply allow this to be; eventually, a great peace will descend.

Anything fully experienced is joy. If you understood this one thing fully, your path to enlightenment would be very short indeed. Conflict fully experienced is joy. Pain fully experienced is joy. Sadness fully experienced is joy. Doubt fully experienced is joy. Anger fully experienced is joy. Happiness fully experienced is joy. Love fully experienced is joy.

When the self disappears, our need to constantly interpret reality disappears with it. When interpretations about reality disappear, we experience reality for what it is, rather than what we would like it to be. Rather than constantly craving what we define as pleasurable experiences, and constantly resisting what we define as unpleasurable experiences, we simply become the experience, moment to moment, of consciousness expressing itself through us.

Enlightenment is both an event and a process. The event corresponds with the dissolution of the sense of a separate self. Beyond this, however, there is a continuously deepening process of oneness.

Moving into oneness is not all bliss. At some point, you should expect to go through an "endarkenment" process, which I discuss in more detail in the forthcoming chapter. This consists of the "dark night of the senses" and the "dark night of the soul." The first is a sustained process of examining the ugliness of the mind. The second is a period of existential emptiness where the contents of the personal unconscious get completely cleaned out. Either of these could be accompanied by feelings of intense loneliness, heaviness, doubt, or despair.

The dark night could be a psychological as well as an existential process. Psychological suffering involves the self, and once the self disappears, so does the suffering. The journey into existential emptiness would be impossible if there were still a sense of personal identity left. When Jesus wrestled with "Satan" in the wilderness, he was clearing out his personal unconsciousness in preparation for his ministry. In his journey into the realms of hell after his Crucifixion, he was clearing out aspects of the collective unconsciousness of humanity.

Not much can be said definitively about this journey, because it will be unique for each individual. It cannot be lengthened or shortened. It is a necessary part of coming into mastery. Bhagavan says that eventually each of us will have to undergo this experience. As we go through this individually, it is possible that it will clear out the collective unconsciousness of humanity to such an extent that it will then become easy for collective enlightenment to happen.

In the more immediate context, Bhagavan refers to three stages of enlightenment: 1) the ability to simply witness life as you disengage from the mind; 2) recognition of the interconnectedness of life; and 3) cosmic oneness. In the first stage, the interference of the mind stops, and your senses come alive. There is the experience of a profound inner silence, and you begin to experience reality as it is. This is what most people experience after the first peak experience of the deeksha. It becomes their new sense of ordinary reality.

In the second stage, you begin to experience a sense of interconnectedness with your immediate world—with nature and with others in the human family. Synchronicities abound and you discover that there is an underlying unity running through all life.

In the third stage, you have moved beyond the sense of interconnectedness to complete union with the cosmos. One moment you are a bird, and then a grasshopper, and then the emptiness of the sky. Here you experience your identity as all there is. You are everything and nothing. "Aham Brahmasmi," said the ancient mystics of India: "I am this whole process called the universe!"

The experience of oneness with the universe is known as samadhi. At first, the experience of samadhi may be fleeting. In order to hold this experience, every nerve cell in the physical and subtle bodies becomes infused with kundalini energy, and it may take some time for the body to integrate these heightened frequencies.

There may even be occasions when the person appears to "die" for short periods, as the functions of the body become short-circuited. In the early stages of enlightenment, a person may experience peak states of samadhi, but this will not last long. As you progress, you experience increasingly longer states of cosmic communion, interspersed with periods of "ordinary" reality.

The ancient yogis describe four stages of samadhi. The first stage is known as *savikalpa* samadhi. There is an experience of oneness with the universe, vibrant bliss, and an activation of the subtle senses. Various inner gifts and abilities may open up. This downpour of new energy is refreshingly ecstatic, but can be quite overwhelming to the nervous system, which eventually returns to a more operational frequency. This is the peak state that many people experience when they first receive the deeksha.

As the nervous system becomes adjusted to the increased flow of kundalini moving through the body, it eventually becomes ready for the next stage of samadhi, known as *nirvikalpa* samadhi. Here, the consciousness gets drawn upward into a unified state of consciousness, while the physical body goes through an extreme shift. Remaining for hours or even days in catatonic states resembling death, every cell of the body becomes transfused with light. This is a relatively nonfunctional state.

Eventually, you move to the third stage of samadhi, called *sahaja* samadhi. The *nadis* and cells of the physical body have now become accustomed to the heightened frequencies of enlightenment, and it is possible to live in the permanent state of unified awareness while being fully functional in daily life.

Bhagavan remarks that the enlightenment that he gives is one where the recipient is intended to be fully functional. Therefore, he is attempting to modify the nervous system so that people require less time in nirvikalpa samadhi and move sooner into sahaja samadhi. This is the state that masters, such as Jesus, operated from. It requires that the unconscious mind be completely cleared, and the adept may consequently go through a prolonged dark night of the soul before this state is permanently anchored.

There is a fourth stage of samadhi, and has been relatively rare in human history so far. Known as *soruba* samadhi, the physical body becomes so infused with higher energies that it becomes a body of light. The mind is now in complete service to the soul, and the adept is now capable of bodily experiencing any dimension of space and time. This stage is sometimes known as ascension, and it is the state that ascended masters, such as Babaji, Kuthumi, and St. Germaine, exhibit.

These masters have chosen to remain close to the earth dimensions in order to assist humanity, and they still appear in physical bodies when needed. There are also stories of *siddha* masters in south India, as well as Tibetan adepts, who have taken the rainbow body, and simply disappeared in a flash of light. Ramalinga Swami was a well-known example of this from the nineteen century. The work of Sri Aurobindo and the Mother was also related to this.

An avatar's job is to make possible what hasn't been possible before. The world is a dream in the mind of God, and an avatar's job, as a divine incarnation, is to exhibit certain states of consciousness in order to open up the same possibilities for the rest of humanity. This is what Bhagavan's mission is. In time, as more and more people experience these possibilities within their own bodies, it will lead to a mutation within the genetic structure of the human species, just as with the "hundredth monkey" (see glossary).

All consciousness is a field. The mind is a field. The enlightened state is also a field. Rupert Sheldrake, a British biologist, referred to these fields of consciousness as "morphogenetic fields" or "form-generating fields." These are the fields that have shaped our evolution, shaped our memories, and shaped our biological forms. Every time one of these morphogenetic fields gets reinforced, it gets stronger. Every time someone "unplugs" from one of these fields, it gets weaker.

This means that every time another person unplugs from the matrix of the mind, the ancient mind becomes weaker. Every time another person becomes enlightened, the morphogenetic fields of enlightenment become stronger, making it easier for everybody else to become enlightened. These two fields are in a see-saw relationship with each other: When one is up, the other is down. Soon will come a time when critical mass will be reached, swinging the entire human consciousness into the state of enlightenment. Once this happens, a new species of humanity will emerge.

U.S. psychiatrist David Hawkins has written a fascinating book, *Power vs. Force*, on this theme. Using the science of kinesiology, he devised a consciousness scale going from 0 to 1,000. On the bottom end of the scale are highly charged negative emotions, such as guilt, shame, terror, and rage, and their corresponding states of consciousness. On the upper end of the scale are love, joy, and various states of enlightenment.

Hawkins discovered that one person who was vibrating at the higher end of this scale could offset thousands, even millions of people, who were vibrating at the lower end of this scale. He also affirmed that one avatar vibrating at 1,000 could offset an entire Planetary Mind hell-bent on extinction!

Perhaps avatars such as Amma and Bhagavan vibrate at 1,000, or at least very close to it. It is based on this principle of resonant fields that Bhagavan says mass enlightenment can happen. When a person becomes enlightened, his consciousness makes a huge leap on this consciousness scale, which directly affects all consciousness in the surrounding area. When the number of enlightened people reaches a critical point, the morphogenetic field of enlightenment will counterbalance the morphogenetic field of the ancient mind, making it possible for mass enlightenment to take place within a very short time.

There is nothing in life that I can think of that could be more exciting or meaningful than this!

23.

Journey of Endarkenment

We have received the deeksha. We have had our first taste of enlightenment. We have experienced the rush of infinite, divine possibility. We have caught our first vision of an imminent Golden Age. We have seen the big picture, in which all the world's problems have been miraculously solved. We have glimpsed a hope in our psyches that spells freedom from a lifetime of suffering. We have fallen in love with the infinite possibilities of being.

Then, suddenly, comes the reality check. The wave of enlightenment is suddenly churning backward, as the ocean inevitably pulls back toward itself, and all our dreams suddenly dissolve in the foam. There is a great turbulence. It is a time of testing and agony. No longer are we experiencing divine ecstasy. We watch helplessly as our fondest dreams begin to collapse all around us. The universe suddenly seems to have forgotten all about us, or even seems to have turned against us. We wonder if we have been given a false vision, or if the universe makes any sense anymore. We find ourselves being pounded into the sand and churned around by the universe-ocean until all that is left is a blind sense of betrayal and despair.

Eventually, we break through this sense of soul pounding, and we enter into an altogether new realm of mastery. The last remnants of the ego's attachment to separation dissolve, and we are free. But how do we get from here to there?

St. John of the Cross, an early Christian mystic, coined the term "dark night of the soul." In my early twenties, when I was going through bouts of tremendous depression, I came across his book and found myself fascinated. It seemed that every word was written just for me, and it helped me understand what was going on from a different perspective. I would like to share a few reflections here on what St. John's words might mean for us at this point in our journey.

St. John refers to two distinct processes, which have surface similarities, but are actually quite different from each other. The first process is what he calls the "dark night of the senses." Later on in the book, he describes the "dark night of the soul." I refer to them both together as our journey into endarkenment.

I would like to distinguish here between these two events. Most of us have experienced feelings of great loneliness, emotional dryness, and depression. Sometimes these states come and go; other times they remain for weeks or months, or even years, at a time. Much of this is a psychological process. We feel unworthy, small, unloved, and insecure. The universe feels too big and too frightening for us to handle, and we find ourselves retreating from it into an increasingly tinier box in order to feel secure. We feel lost and cut off from other people. We feel too inadequate to live out our dreams. We have been hurt by life and by other people, and we retreat into a cave of our own making, alternating between feelings of anger, betrayal, helplessness, loneliness, sadness, and grief.

Dealing with our unhealed psychological issues is often painful, and the deeksha can accelerate this process as it pushes us toward wholeness. All this is part of the dark night of the senses. Often, we find that the brighter the light that shines upon us, the deeper the darkness that gets stirred up.

When I lived in Mt. Shasta, California, there was a lake that I would frequently visit. It was a shallow lake, and the bottom half of it was squishy mud. I loved walking through it, stirring up all the bubbles of methane gas from the muck at the bottom, watching as they made their way up to the surface to be released.

The psychological process is similar to this. We see, for the first time, some of our shadow aspects, which have been buried in the mud for so long. We have tried to suppress, deny, or project these things for a long time, but they are still there. What do we do with these bubbles of subconscious material that get stirred up?

Very often we try to suppress or deny these feelings, memories, or sensations once again. They are uncomfortable, and don't fit with our ideas of wanting to be spiritually enlightened beings. Or else we go into depression or contraction, and then feel guilty or ashamed for what we perceive as failure or unworthiness. A third thing that we might do is to project these feelings onto other people or circumstances, actively or passively blaming them for our own feelings of darkness and discomfort. This is especially true for those who have experienced significant hurt or abuse in their early childhood. The need to blame oneself or somebody else can get intensely strong, to compensate for all the shadows that the deeksha begins to push toward the surface.

If we no longer want to get into old patterns of suppression, denial, or projection, there is a fourth option. We can simply watch and observe this process. We don't need to try to change anything. If we are willing to hold still and stay with the feelings, the bubbles from the mud will naturally come up to the surface of the lake, and get released. However, when we actively go into suppression, denial, or projection, we halt the process and become stuck in the dark night. This is where many people have felt lost or betrayed, feeling as though somehow the deeksha hasn't worked for them, or that they are worse off than ever before.

If we can allow ourselves to go through the dark night of the senses, simply experiencing the reality of the mind as it is, it soon passes. More light can then come in, and deeper experiences of oneness can begin to permeate our lives. We discover a stronger connection with our inner divinity—the antaryamin—and a greater sense of our unique destiny as a soul on earth.

At some point of this journey, another transformative crisis begins. This is the dark night of the soul. Whereas the dark night of the senses is a psychological crisis, the dark night of the soul is an existential crisis. Whereas the purpose of the dark night of the senses is to dissolve the sense of a separate self, leading to enlightenment, the purpose of the dark night of the soul is to discover the divine Self, and enter into God-realization.

The inner experience may be similar. There is again the sense of great loneliness, emotional dryness, and depression. But this time, it is the experience of the inner soul, not the outer personality. Often we feel that our very connection with the Divine is broken, there is no more joy in our hearts, and everything that had been so smooth and easy on our spiritual path is now burdensome and difficult.

Why is this happening? This is where the last and subtlest shreds of the personal ego are being confronted. Our certainties and sense of ultimate purpose are being challenged. We are being pushed into the void, where everything that has to do with our last remaining ideas and concepts about divinity, truth, and ultimate reality dissolves. Even our ideas about the big picture get eaten up in the void. It feels as though it is a dismemberment of our very being, a journey through the Valley of Death. The journey feels endless, and just when we finally surrender to this death, we emerge reborn as a Christ being.

This is the stage that Jesus went through in his "forty days in the wilderness." As he struggled with the remnants of his inner demons, he was able to dissolve the last illusions of a separate self, and merge with the "Father," his inner divinity. This was when he became the Christ. This was when his mission as an avatar could truly begin.

We are on this same journey. Bhagavan makes it clear that we are all an aspect of the collective avatar, which is descending on earth. He emphasizes the need to go through our own dark night of the soul, and challenges us to step into our mastery. This is, he says, what it takes to hold the light for others to step into.

Do not confuse the dark night of the senses with the dark night of the soul. Just because we are feeling miserable does not mean we are automatically moving into mastery. The journey has begun, however. The way through both of these dark nights is the same. We must simply become aware of our inner process without judging or blaming. And we must trust that this divine intelligence is with us as much in the darkness as in the light. When we can finally surrender fully to the perfection of God within the darkness, we mysteriously discover that we have emerged once again into the light!

When we emerge from the dark night of the senses, we step more fully into oneness. When we emerge from the dark night of the soul, we step more fully into mastery. We become God-realized, and can serve humanity as part of the collective avatar on earth, one cell in a planetary body as it slowly builds the critical mass necessary to achieve the collective planetary awakening!

Some Christian mystics referred to this as the cloud of unknowing. At first, God steps toward us and gives us an experience of sweetness. Then, a cloud of unknowing comes between us. It is up to us to step through it, undefining all our concepts of God, however dry and stark this feels as we struggle with all our doubts and uncertainties, until we step out of the cloud of the unconscious mind, and discover that God's grace has indeed never left. We now experience ourselves as one with God.

Those of us who have not experienced this unity with God conceptualize God as mechanistic and separate from us. It is a belief held within the unconscious. In order to truly experience oneness with God, we must go through the dark night of the unconscious mind, which I see as our personal version of the ancient mind. Once we have cleared this, nothing in the ancient mind can influence us anymore. Then we become the power of God to heal, help, and liberate humanity from suffering. Then we become a Christ.

Christ was about love. This love is what gave Jesus the power to heal people. This is what the deeksha is creating within us. We do not gain the ability to love by trying to develop love. It happens by itself as the deeksha begins clearing out the unconscious mind.

I sense that the cycles of enlightenment and endarkenment that each of us will be going through in this passage toward oneness are the same cycles that collective humanity will be going through in these years to come. It is the same cycles that our beloved Mother Earth is going through as She prepares to birth humanity and all life into a Golden Age. Despite appearances, there is a huge, omnipotent, loving Intelligence that is working through all of this.

It seems to me that we may now be collectively entering a cycle of endarkenment. From what people tell me, and from indications within the Mayan calendar and other prophetic systems, I have concluded that perhaps something is coming to a head on a planetary level, a big collective process that is now beginning or about to happen. What this would look like, I do not know and cannot say. But I recognize that the divine Grace that is pouring into the earth today is beyond all temporal forms and cannot be diminished or held back by anything.

Sri Aurobindo, the great mystic sage of India, referred to this collective endarkenment as the "supramental catastrophe," and noted that there would inevitably be a period of transition where all our collective shadows would surface. My sense is that this is about to peak on our planet in these coming months and years. Yet he also stated that this would be followed by the "supramental manifestation," what Bhagavan calls the dawning of the Golden Age.

So if you are currently experiencing the dark night, remember the big picture. Know that no matter what stage of the process you are going through, there is a gift of grace alive in you, which will continue working within you and through you forever. If you stay in a state of openness, allowing the storm winds to blow through you without resistance, you will come out the other side of this with a deepened capacity to serve the One. The "fire from heaven" will have burned away the remnants of separation. You will have experienced your true face, which has nothing to do with the face that you have learned to recognize in the mirrors of daily life.

In the words of an ancient Indian prayer, "Lead us from untruth into truth. Lead us from darkness into light. Lead us from death into immortality!"

Long, Dark Night

Desolate winds howl in icy winter night.
The pilgrim stops in his endless wanderings,
And lends his own voice to the wind.
How can it be when the sky is emptied
When nothing remains to obscure the sun,
That life is strangely fed in this mystic darkness?
The silent vastness ebbs and flows.
These riches can only be seen
By one whose eyes are empty of seeing,
When the fires of desolation
Have flared up and then died away,
When the last embers of hope and certainty
Have faded in the night.
How can it be, my Friend,
That I hear you so clearly now
When everything I have ever known
Has smoldered away with these embers?
The storms of separation have passed,
Only the wet snow bears witness.
The dark night is revealed
As doorway to deepest light.
I have found my voice
In the softly running, silent living,
Wild pulsing heart
Of Eternity!

24.

Vision of the Golden Age

A question I had often asked myself was, *Are we birthing a Golden Age or are we spiraling into extinction?* If we were to look only at the outer physical realities, we would have to say that we are in extreme global crisis. Where does hope lie for our planet?

Near the beginning of the twentieth century, the great Indian freedom fighter and yogi-sage Sri Aurobindo began to express a truth that had not been expressed before. In his high states of divine union, he saw that the time had come for a new stage in the evolution of humanity. He saw that the Divine was to manifest right here on earth and that the time for this divine emergence into earth life was now. He spoke of heaven descending to earth, even as earth experienced a breakdown because of its intrinsic resistance to this descent.

Sri Aurobindo was joined in Pondicherry, India, by a French mystic, Mirra Alfassa, who later became known as the Mother. Together, they embarked on a journey of intensive cellular transformation that is very relevant to Bhagavan's mission of planetary enlightenment.

Grace and I had spent time in Auroville, the international city founded on the vision of Sri Aurobindo and the Mother. Like Amma and Bhagavan, they, too, perceived themselves to be a single avataric consciousness in two bodies. They considered their own mission to be that of bringing what they called the "supramental force" down to the level of physical matter.

Bhagavan himself acknowledges "the incomparable work of Sri Aurobindo and the Mother," and says that without their efforts, his own mission would not be possible. Interestingly, Amma's birthday is the same as Sri Aurobindo's birthday, and Bhagavan and the Mother are both Pisces! Sri Aurobindo left his body shortly after Bhagavan was born. Was he waiting to pass the torch along to Bhagavan before he died?

What is this supramental force that Sri Aurobindo and the Mother talk about? What is it that they accomplished? As I speak about their accomplishments, I am now speaking not only from their writings or their teachings, which can be found easily elsewhere, but from what I sense in my own body after my experience of cosmic consciousness.

Sri Aurobindo refers to the supramental force as a divine energy that is descending down into physical matter. Most people think of matter as the ultimate expression of the field of duality, as if divine consciousness were at the top of a metaphoric ladder and physical consciousness were at the very bottom. Divine consciousness is somehow considered to be a unified field, while matter exists in separation consciousness. We tend to think of ourselves as separate individuals in the field of matter.

The field of quantum physics informs us that what we call matter is mostly empty space. Quantum physicists tell us that the foundation of all matter in the universe is a subatomic particle, the quark. In fact, some theoretical physicists claim that the entire universe is but a single quark, continually replicating itself in parallel dimensions of space and time. Therefore, they say, all matter is related; the appearance of the separate existence of matter is an illusion of perception.

It is not matter that is illusion, as many spiritual seekers believe, but our perception of matter that is illusion! Quantum mechanics has nothing to do with how small a world we are talking about. It is the size of our consciousness that counts; it alone determines whether we live by clear-cut, consensus-based Newtonian laws or an infinite range of quantum possibilities.

How do you translate the richness of these holographic quantum possibilities into a tasteless, senseless, language-based world of linear mind in linear time? I had an experience of this once when I was swimming in Hawaii with a mother and baby humpback whale, and was taken inside the mother's consciousness to see how she was able to embrace all of Earth within her body. I realized that whales are not restricted by linear reality. Their brains are formulated to perceive the world from a much more holistic perspective, a perspective in which the boundaries of separate matter dissolve, a perspective which mystics, yogis, and shamans also share.

I recall the vision that Grace had in which Shiva was offering her the cosmic egg. What happens when we crack open the cosmic egg? What happens when we enter the quantum worlds where science and spirituality speak the same language, where the physical and mystical worlds are revealed to be the same? Will we follow the long spiral of eternity back to its source? Or will we recognize that perhaps the egg never existed apart from the universe, and that we were never separate from the source to begin with!

The illusion of separate existence is the legacy of the ancient mind. We are conditioned to believe that this is so, and therefore we experience our consciousness as being somehow trapped in matter. The morphogenetic field of our biological species responds to this shared belief by producing the limitations of matter that we are familiar with: sickness, aging, and death.

What if this could be changed? What if the unified field that Sri Aurobindo referred to as supramental consciousness could be brought down into the morphogenetic fields of the earth in order to completely alter our relationship with matter? This, as I see it, was the work of Sri Aurobindo and the Mother. Quantum theory tells us that all matter is essentially one. If they could bring the supramental force down into their own bodies, it would have an equal impact upon the morphogenetic fields of all matter on earth.

They referred to unified matter as "true matter," and felt that if they succeeded in bringing this supramental force down into their own bodies—changing their bodies into true matter—the supramental force would eventually work through the morphogenetic fields of humanity into all human bodies. A new supramental species would emerge. They succeeded in their effort to bring the supramental force into their bodies, and believed that the supramental force would most assuredly descend into human consciousness in years to come.

Bhagavan says that when mass enlightenment takes place, the ancient mind will become powerless. When this happens, our perceptions of reality will undergo a huge shift. We will no longer be bound by the laws of classical physics. We will begin to experience quantum reality in our bodies. Is this the same as Aurobindo's vision of the descent of supramental consciousness?

I believe that Bhagavan's work is to take this force that is now established in the supramental fields of the earth, and to make it available to every person on earth. It is significant to me that the Matrimandir, which the Mother designed as the focus through which the supramental force would descend on earth, is shaped like a golden sphere. Is there a connection between this and the golden sphere that Bhagavan has programmed to descend into the crown chakra of the person who has received the deeksha?

Sri Aurobindo said that a supramental species was to be born on earth, which would be as different from humanity today as we are from cavepeople. Is this the process that will be initiated once the ancient mind is dissolved and the Golden Age is born? In Sri Aurobindo's epic poem *Savitri*, he vividly describes this new race of humanity:

> *I saw them cross the twilight of an age,*
> *The sun-eyed children of a marvelous dawn,*
> *Great creators with wide brows of calm,*
> *The massive barrier-breakers of the world,*
> *Laborers in the quarries of the gods*
> *The architects of immortality.*
> *Into the fallen human sphere they came,*
> *Faces that wore the Immortal's glory still . . .*
> *Bodies made beautiful by the spirit's light . . .*
> *Carrying the Dionysian cup of joy,*
> *Lips chanting an unknown anthem of the soul,*
> *Feet echoing in the corridors of Time.*
> *High priests of wisdom, sweetness, might, and bliss;*
> *Discoverers of beauty's sunlit ways . . .*
> *Their tread one day shall change the suffering earth*
> *And justify the light on Nature's face. (Savitri, pp. 343–4)*

Our collective experience of reality is shaped by the ancient mind. Because it is our shared reality, we consider it to be the only possible reality. We cannot conceive of stepping outside this ancient mind to consider that other realities might exist. Until we are enlightened, we cannot begin to conceive that we can create any reality we choose, through the infinite creative power of the universe.

Have you seen *The Matrix*? In this movie, earth has been taken over by machines. Humans are cloned in breeding tanks, and their central nervous systems are tapped in order to provide the machines with the energy needed for their own functioning. In order to lull humans into a false sense of purpose and security, however, an entire mass holographic reality has been created for the cloned humans, so that they appear to themselves to be eating, sleeping, working, watching TV, making love, and otherwise living normal lives.

This is the matrix, and it is policed by agents who ensure that nobody comes to realize their true state of being. It is only when Neo, the archetypal hero, is unplugged from the matrix that he recognizes the extent of his captivity, and the madness of his former existence. With the help of his mentor, Morpheus, he slowly learns that he can create his own reality outside the matrix, a reality no longer subject to the rules of the matrix. In fact, the only limits are the limits of his own imagination. Once he discovers this, the agents have no more power over him, and he is free.

In a very real sense, the ancient mind is the matrix. It creates an illusory sense of reality based on the shared assumptions of all those trapped within it. It is filled with fear, ugliness, and suffering. It is programmed to consider the body as separate. In its belief in separation, it utilizes the principle of entropy, which says that all energy winds down into chaos, ultimately leading to death. Nobody questions its existence. The agents of social conditioning, ignorance, and self-doubt ensure that nobody attempts to win her way to freedom. Yes, we might have all kinds of ideas and concepts about freedom, but all these are inside the matrix as well.

Enlightenment is about unplugging from the matrix! Once we recognize how we are programmed by the ancient mind, we cannot help but break free. When mass enlightenment happens, our collective sense of ego separation will dissolve. When this happens, we will instantly be freed from the conditioning and karma inherent within the ancient mind. Like Neo, we will discover as a species that we can break past our perceived limitations to create any reality we wish. It will be a dance of creation and freedom never before experienced. This, I believe, is what the Golden Age will be about.

"Humanity is entering the most crucial phase of its existence," says Bhagavan. "The coming decade will witness the most unprecedented and undreamed-of changes in the course of its long evolution. There is nothing much humanity can do about it, other than to understand the changes that are overpowering it. Toward the end of this phase, humanity will enter a new age: the Golden Age!"

IV

Conversation with Bhagavan

Conversation with Bhagavan

This is the transcript of a conversation that I had with Bhagavan on October 8, 2004, in Golden City. We discuss issues of personal and global enlightenment through the deeksha, which is an electrical transmission of divine energy. Those who receive the deeksha undergo neurobiological changes in the brain, leading to states of enlightenment. Bhagavan and I also discuss environmental catastrophes and earth changes, human death, and the advent of the long-awaited Golden Age. This conversation is also available as a DVD, published by Kosmic Studios, the publishing arm of Oneness University.

Namaste, Bhagavan. I am so grateful for your presence on this earth and in my life, and for the gift of enlightenment that you have given to me, and are giving to the world. For myself, I can say that there really seems like there is no individual self left, that who I am is simply the universe expressing through this body, experiencing itself moment to moment in a very fresh way. It seems like there is an emptiness here, an emptiness that is, at the same time, very full . . .

For the readers of my book and for people watching this video, I would first like to ask you to introduce yourself . . .

Well, I am known in India as Bhagavan. I am an avatar, an avatar who is specifically concerned about enlightening people and, of course, also fulfilling their desires. I have been around for the past nearly twelve years or so. We have millions of followers, and a few thousand now who are enlightened. We can say that there is some kind of spiritual renaissance going on in the country here. We have been able to address all sections of society: men and women, young and old, rich and poor. There is now a tremendous seeking after enlightenment, a great passion now among large numbers of people to become enlightened, and so I have come to be considered as an avatar for enlightenment.

Bhagavan, for those who may not be familiar with the term avatar, *how would you define it?*

In India, we have this concept of the avatar. An avatar could be a musical avatar, a mathematical avatar, a political avatar, or a spiritual avatar. An avatar is someone who comes with a specific mission on the planet and who is divinely inspired, and through whom divine energies flow. Avatars can come in every field of human activity. Many seem to think it can only pertain to spiritual work, but it isn't so. But I happen to be a spiritual avatar.

You and Amma, your wife, are both avatars?

Yes we are both avatars, like two sides of the same coin. We have excellent understanding and communication, and sometimes we don't even have to talk to know what's going on. We work like one being when it comes to enlightenment and helping people.

Bhagavan, there have been so many avatars in human history, who have come and given different teachings, and helped to maybe enlighten a few people. What makes you so different?

Well, I think it is not about my being different. I think I have
come at a different time. The other avatars prepared people for
enlightenment, for liberation, but could not give it to them, not
because they were not capable of giving it, but because the times
were not ready for that. So I come at a time when earth's energies have changed, and man is very receptive, and it is possible
to give him enlightenment. So my advantage is that I have come
at the right time, a time when it is possible to give it to man.

*Does this have something to do with our movement into the
Golden Age?*

It definitely has to do with the emergence of the Golden Age.
In India, it is believed that the Kali Yuga started sometime
around 3002 B.C. and is supposed to have ended in A.D. 2002
By 2003, we are right into the Golden Age. That's why we
began giving enlightenment publicly in the year 2003.

So it's only been one year.

It's only been one year.

*How do you give enlightenment? How is it possible to give
enlightenment?*

Ah yes. Basically, it is through the process of what is called
deeksha, an electrical energy which transfers through some
kind of a hole in the mind of man. We believe that the mind
of man is like a wall, which divides man from God. The deeksha is an electrical energy which makes a hole in this wall,

which we call the mind. Once that happens, then God and man can come to relate with each other. The way they relate has to do with his background, his conditioning, his aspirations, his education, so many factors. But it is God who gives enlightenment, whether you call it God or Cosmic Consciousness or nature, call it what you want. . . . So that takes over and enlightenment is delivered through God. He is the one who delivers. Our job is to give the deeksha and make a hole in the mind, and then God does the rest. It's a very complex process that only God can do.

Is this something you have been preparing for, for a very long time?

Yes, my whole life has been a preparation for this. Ever since I was a child, my only concern was how to liberate man from his suffering. These were not things that I arrived at through my own life experience, because I myself was a child, but rather I was forced to become concerned about man's suffering and to work for that. That is why I am an avatar, because I never arrived at these conclusions: I was just led into these things by a higher energy, a higher force, what you call the Divine Energy, or God.

Ever since I was a child, I was made to do certain practices, which I did for many years. So that has given me the ability. So mostly, I don't give deeksha. I let others give deeksha. I am more like a powerhouse, and the others are like step-down transformers who can receive this energy and pass it on to people. So my function is to remain as a powerhouse for some time. So this is how deeksha is given and how enlightenment or God-realization occurs.

So when you give deeksha—you speak of this deeksha as a neurobiological process that affects the brain?

Yes, when we give deeksha it is like the passing on of an electrical energy that affects the brain, the spinal cord, and what we call the ductless glands, [the physical physiological basis of] the chakras. So most of the work is being done on the frontal lobes and the parietal lobes of the brain. There is an activation of the frontal lobes, and a deactivation of the parietal lobes, plus some energies are sent into the ductless glands to reactivate these chakras. So all this, in turn, produces a hole in the mind, and a link is established between God and man. Thereafter, what happens is God's work. Up to then, of course, we can do certain things.

Right. So when you speak about losing the "self," that's what happens when you make this hole in the wall.

When you make the hole in the wall, then God can take over, and then he works on the senses, liberating the senses from the mind, from the clutches of the mind. When that happens, you lose your "self." That part of the work happens through God himself. As he is the creator, he works like a computer to rearrange the brain, and he takes over.

So each person's enlightenment is absolutely unique, then.

It's absolutely unique. It depends on his background, his conditioning, what happened in his childhood, his own seeking, his religious conditioning. So all these things are involved.

Bhagavan, many, many people have been seeking for many, many lifetimes, and been through all kinds of practices and sadhanas and rituals and ceremonies and traditions, and many times they feel they have only been able to go so far, and none have been able to actually cross over into enlightenment. So how is this different?

When I look at a person, I don't see him as a first-timer. I only see millions of years behind him. I believe that all of humanity has finished all the work they need to do. I think everybody has been well prepared through so many lives. And therefore, now is the time to get it. All the hard work has been done. I believe everybody has done the hard work, and now the fruit is there to be had.

Yes, it must be such a relief for many people to hear that.

Yes, that's why I see everyone as a seeker. Everybody has done their sadhana; everybody is ready. I cannot say so-and-so is not ready.

So there's no one who is not a seeker?

There is no one who is not a seeker. They could be seeking in different ways . . .

They could be seeking without even knowing they are seeking.

Without knowing they are seeking . . .

So as this work progresses, is it possible that more and more people will become enlightened who have no idea about enlightenment, who have never been seeking enlightenment, it will simply just happen?

Yes, what is likely to happen is that there are now people who are enlightened who are able to give deeksha to people who are able to get into good states. But very soon, maybe a few months from now, those who will receive deeksha from them will naturally become enlightened. And not only that, they will be able to give deeksha to others and make them enlightened. This process will continue for some time. There will come a time when, without deeksha, the whole of mankind is going to make it. Once the critical level is reached, there is going to be a spontaneous occurrence across the planet.

What will this look like in practical terms?

In practical terms, the world will look very different. We will not be able to talk about me being an Indian or you being an American or somebody else being an African. We cannot talk in terms of races and nationalities or I can't say, *I'm a Hindu, I'm a Christian, I'm a Muslim.*

So all these things which divide man will just disappear. All these things will just drop off. There will be no need for these things. All these divisions will not exist. We will become just human beings. We will become one family. It's not a concept: This will just happen. This is when we will truly become humans. But as long as we are going to define ourselves in terms of nationalities, religions, cultures, races, we will still continue to be tribal and very primitive. We are becoming human now. It will definitely happen.

What about people who are still into power, control, and ego games, and who may not want to get enlightened?

Yes, people who stubbornly resist enlightenment will also naturally become enlightened. At that point, there won't be any resisting it. Nobody can say, *I will stay out of enlightenment.* That is not possible. It's a natural occurrence. It's human evolution. So all these power games and ego games will just stop. You can just not do it anymore. The brain will function differently.

That's amazing. So even the people who are consciously and adamantly refusing to even think about sharing the earth with other people, who are trying to control the resources of the earth and creating environmental devastation for their own benefit, whether companies, governments, businesses, or individuals, this will all change?

Yes, all this will dramatically change. Man will soon realize that the earth is a living organism, he depends on it like his mother, so no one will even think of harming the earth. This won't take some kind of education: It will be a natural happening. This is what will happen. So we are going to see a very different earth, a very different world. I am not speculating. I am just speaking very directly from the visions thousands of people have had in the last decade from various continents.

Bhagavan, there are many scientists who predict, based on what is happening on the planet today—global warming, a possible ice age coming, the quality of air and water, and so on—that there could be a major environmental catastrophe, and that we might even end up wiping out all life on the planet. How can you be so sure that there will be a planetary enlightenment?

The predictions are quite true, but what they are not aware of is that, as we have seen in our visions, a great transformation is sweeping across the planet which will, in turn, prevent these things from happening. Already we are seeing signs of people becoming enlightened, and how it affects the environment. We are able to see this on a very small scale. And from that, we are able to predict that on a global scale this transformation is going to occur. This is what is going to save the earth. If that does not happen, then what the scientists are predicting could very well come true.

So an example could be that if a village gets enlightened, and there has been a drought for the past few years, then the monsoons . . .

The monsoons will come, yes. It is happening in many places in India. We are seeing it.

So similarly, when there are predictions of major earthquakes, volcanic activity, pole shifts even, then, as people become enlightened, this will alter our relationship with the earth . . .

We could save the earth. That is why we are telling people, *The house is on fire: Let us move faster, let us hurry up!*

Yes, this is a very important message for people to hear. There are so many people in despair and hopelessness, so many good people who have given up any kind of future for the earth because of what they see with their outer eyes.

Yes, but there is no need for them to lose hope. Because things are going to change dramatically. In a very unexpected way, things are going to change.

Yes, I am so happy to hear that. As people become enlightened, and as the planet becomes enlightened as a collective, how will that change the physical quality of the earth?

There is a very close correlation between human consciousness and the physical process occurring on the planet. So the moment that conflict levels are reduced in human consciousness, you will find dramatic changes at the earth level also. So you will find a reduction of insects and pests in the crops, and nature behaving in a much better way without the need for chemicals. All these things are a natural consequence of the reduction of conflict in human consciousness. There is such a close correlation between the two. This also we are seeing on a small scale at the village level.

So as humans become enlightened, then our relationship with the environment will change, species that have become extinct will come back, the oceans will become depolluted, and so on.

Yes, we have seen remarkable things happening on a small scale, so we believe it can happen on a large scale also. So that's why we are so confident that these things will happen. Otherwise, there seems to be no hope in living at all.

Yes, otherwise there doesn't seem to be any point in going on. Bhagavan, one question I have is about your and Amma's consciousness, which pervades the deeksha. How is it possible, with so many people receiving the deeksha now, that you are able to track what's happening with everybody individually?

We actually function on two levels. When I am having this conversation with you, certain things are switched off, so that I can hold this meaningful conversation. But at other times, the switches are on and we can experience a lot of human beings at once and what is going on in their minds and their consciousness, and we can interfere and do many things. That dimension is not known to man. I am not claiming this as something special to me, because whatever I am experiencing, I believe in making others also experience, and there are also others now at that level who can similarly experience a few hundred beings at the same time. This is a faculty that is very natural to man and will start to open up in many people. To me, it happens very naturally. Because of what happened to me in my early life, I can focus on a 100,000-strong crowd and go into them and do many things.

So you are able to go into the collective consciousness . . .

Yes, it happens very easily and very naturally. And others, too, are now able to do it to some extent. Soon, it will start happening in a bigger way.

And that's very much a part of enlightenment.

That's very much a part of enlightenment. In fact, many things will start happening after enlightenment. We are not talking very much about it because it is going to happen very naturally. Enlightenment is not going to stop at just being aware of things, or just being joyful or being in bliss. There is a lot more to it. But these will follow in the months coming.

One question which may sound a little strange: How is your consciousness as an avatar different from the consciousness of someone who gets enlightened?

At this point in time, the only difference could be in the intensity of the awareness or the intensity of the bliss, but otherwise there is no basic, fundamental difference. But as these *nadis* open up and become stronger, his awareness levels will also increase and the gap will soon close. But it may take a little time. But fundamentally, there is no difference. Except I do have some additional facilities. Like I can see what is going on in some other place, what's happening in somebody's mind, how I can help them. I can really interfere in helping their life by taking up a strong sankalpa, a strong wish. These, too, people will be able to acquire in the course of time. Already a few of them have acquired this, in small measure.

So as people deepen into their enlightenment, these will be things that anyone is capable of?

Yes, as your concern for people grows, these things naturally start happening. It's all a matter of how concerned you are about others. As you go deeper and deeper into enlightenment, your concern also increases. Along with this, these things also start happening.

Yes, it seems as if an entirely new species is arising.

Yes, it's more like that, an entirely new species is emerging.

Bhagavan, there are so many different religions in the world today. What is your attitude toward all the different faiths?

I believe that different religions are required to handle the different needs of people. I have seen people sometimes require a particular religion to handle a particular problem, or their background needs the input of a particular religion. I personally have never had any difficulty with people of any faith.

Because the deeksha is a neutral thing and the deeksha only activates a certain area of the brain or deactivates it, and the person only discovers what his religion taught him. So he discovers the truths of his own faith. What I do or teach is not a new faith or religion. It is not anything new at all. It merely helps you to discover what you have been seeking all these years. So I personally have no conflict with the people of any faith.

So once people are enlightened, the Muslim will experience his unity with Allah, the Christian will experience himself a Christ, a Buddhist will experience Buddha consciousness, and so on?

And so on. There is absolutely no conflict at all. That's why I am saying that soon there will be no divisions of man, saying I belong to this religion or that religion, you know. We are going to become one family. This is going to be a reality.

There is this beautiful song by John Lennon where he speaks of that.

Yes, and we are seeing this happening, especially in the areas where we are working. We are seeing it happening.

Yes, it seems that the differences between religions have only to do with ego, nothing to do with the essence of that religion.

Yes.

Bhagavan, you speak of different stages, different aspects of enlightenment. You speak of the flowering of the heart, you speak of the witness consciousness, you speak about oneness. Could you describe this in more detail?

Yes, the first thing that often happens in the process of enlightenment is the flowering of the heart. You, for the first time, discover real compassion, real love for human beings. But as this becomes deeper, you lose a sense of separateness. Even at this point, we really do not call you fully enlightened. We call you fully enlightened only when you are experiencing reality as it is. To experience reality as it is, these are some kinds of prerequisites. Very rarely, it happens suddenly, in a big way. So these may be called stages of enlightenment. Enlightenment itself is experiencing reality as it is.

Is that equivalent to oneness?

It is equivalent to oneness. But, of course, oneness itself just takes off from there and finally becomes oneness with God, or oneness with Cosmic Consciousness. It is the ultimate oneness. But that could be difficult for some people, to say that man and God could become one. That, some people may not accept, but it is a reality that people can become one with God.

You speak of designing your own God. What do you mean by that?

When I speak of designing your own God, I do not mean that you create your own God. God is someone who creates you, and you do not create God. But the way he is going to treat you and the way he is going to conduct himself with you depends on how you expect him to conduct himself with you. This is taken from the Hindu concept of *bhakta paradeena,* that God is dependent on the devotee. So if you want him to be a friend, he behaves like a friend. If you want him to behave like a mother, he behaves like a mother. So it is in your hands to design the way he is going to behave with you. That's how I say, you design your own God.

So certain aspects, certain views of God will make it easier to actually receive this gift.

Yes, it can be very easy to receive this gift. If your concept of God is a very friendly one, then you don't even have to pray. You just ask it and he gives it to you. Thousands of people have this kind of relationship. I am only talking about when people have actually achieved it, not before that. So people have made God their friend, a very friendly God. This includes Christians, Muslims, Hindus, people of all faiths.

And God is masculine as well as feminine?

God is masculine as well as feminine, or light or formless. Many have only a formless God. Many have it as just light. Some even have him as both male and female. Each person has complete freedom. It's the individual's choice.

You also speak of designing your own enlightenment.

Your own enlightenment, yes; like, for example, you can design how much of heart you want, or how much of oneness you want, or how much of experiencing your reality you want. Again, it depends on your passion, the kind of books you have read, the kind of seeking you have had.

So it's really the beginning of a lifelong journey or exploration . . .

Exploration, yes. And you can change it also, in the course of time, you can change it. In practice, we find that people achieve different states of enlightenment.

What determines what state of enlightenment a person receives? Does it have to do with karmic factors or does it have to do with your belief systems?

It has a lot to do with your belief systems, closely followed by your karma. Very often it has to do with your belief systems, the kind of conditioning you have gone through. But you can change it if you want to at some point in time, if you feel like it. So that's why I am saying you can design your God, and you can design your enlightenment.

Bhagavan, I remember when I was young, I was very fascinated by the life and teachings of Jesus, and always wondered what it would be like to be born in his times, to be one of his disciples, when he sent them out to go heal the sick and relieve suffering. What is fascinating to me now is that the same kinds of miracles, the same kinds of healings are beginning to happen now with the deekshas and with other circumstances. Would you like to say something about that?

Yes, this is the continuation of that work that Christ left behind. This should have happened, in fact, 2,000 years ago—this transformation of man—but for some reason it got aborted. But now, the same thing has come back. So in the deekshas, people are getting in touch with Christ conscious-ness, especially in the West. They are discovering the same consciousness which Christ was trying to give them. It is no different from that. In fact, I would say that would be true Christianity, as Christ intended it to be.

Yes, Christ said, "I and the Father are One."

Yes.

So from that consciousness, miracles are possible. So as people experience the same consciousness today, the same miracles are being evident.

Yes, exactly.

You mention that there are certain miracles taking place in Orissa.

Yes there is a place in Orissa called Gutagaon, where thousands of people come and get healed. There is another place called Bhimavaram, where surgeries are done on them as they come and lie down in front of the srimurti.

Like miracle surgeries. Like psychic surgeries?

Miracle surgeries, yes. More and more, this will be happening around the country and around the world. These are not miracles that I go and do: They are spontaneous miracles occurring around the planet. I personally do not do any miracles like that. I am not a miracle worker, in that sense.

But you train people to become miracle workers.

Yes, around them, these miracles happen.

So it's really Cosmic Consciousness that allows the miracles to take place. So the fact that this is happening more and more, and that enlightenment is happening more and more, you have spoken about this in relationship to what you have called the "morphogenetic fields." Could you describe that phenomenon?

Yes, for example, this phenomenon is about twelve years old, and we have found that at certain intervals, it becomes more powerful. So what we have discovered is that the more people get that state, it becomes easier for other people to get that state, whether it is in connection with healings or the enlightened state or other states of consciousness. We find that people who come later are getting it more easily and much faster. So obviously, there is a field which is absorbing all this transformation and able to transfer it to others much faster. That's how the morphogenetic fields are really helping. We can see it in action.

There is a psychologist in America, David Hawkins. And he has devised a scale of consciousness from 0 to 1,000. At the bottom end of the scale are emotions like guilt, shame, fear; whereas on the upper end, you have love and joy and enlightenment. What he says is that one person who is holding the state of joy or love or enlightenment can actually counterbalance thousands or even millions of people who are holding the states of guilt, shame, and fear that so many people are stuck in. So what he says is that this is also a morphogenetic field and what is taking place is that because it doesn't take a large number of people, as long as they are high on the consciousness scale, they can actually create a huge wave of enlightenment.

Yes, that's very true. That is the purpose of the sages and saints: they have to counterbalance the other negative energies. That is why we believe that once we have sixty-four thousand people, that will be enough for transforming the whole of mankind.

Why sixty-four thousand?

Somehow, that seems to be the necessary number for making this happen very spontaneously. . . . These are factors which have been revealed to us. We don't fully understand the dynamics, but these were revealed to us. We go on the basis of revelation. It is not just something that comes to one person, but if it is something that happens to many people over a long period of time, that is what we accept as revelation. That becomes our road map.

How long will it take to get sixty-four thousand people enlightened?

It could take anywhere from one year to six years. It can happen very fast also. It depends on how quickly people respond. It could happen in a few months' time also. So we can't really specify the time here. It can happen very fast, or it can take a little more time.

So now you are training people to give deekshas themselves, and this will be a part of this. They will move out across the earth and they will begin to give deekshas and make people enlightened. And then eventually, like you said, it will happen through a touch, a glance, a prayer . . .

It could happen very, very fast. Let's say, people read your book. That could be some kind of deeksha. Or they can flock to your talks or programs where you are giving deeksha, and it could happen very, very fast. It can happen very fast, really. People must be very serious. That's all that is required.

I know some musicians who have gone through the deeksha training, and so as they perform the music, then that itself could be a deeksha.

Yes. And one thing likely to happen, as people read your book, they could also get some kind of deeksha. That's also very much possible.

I notice that when I was writing the book, it was flowing through in such an amazing fashion. The entire book was written in ten days. In fact, I felt your presence coming through so strongly. So I am sure it is a deeksha.

Yes, it is more like our architect who designed our Oneness Temple. It just flowed through him, and in no time at all, it was ready. It was just lying before him.

You said about the Oneness Temple, that when people go in to worship, people can come in from any religious faith, but what they will see is a reflection of their own God.

Yes, it is a very strange temple, and there will be a strange throne there, an empty throne. And when people from any faith will come and worship, they will see their God or a sign of their God's presence on the throne. It will only be visible to them. They can pray in any fashion they want. And they will see their God on the throne. That's what is so unique about it.

So it is an inner revelation. It also reminds me of the phenomenon that is growing, known as the phala deeksha. *What actually happens?*

In phala deeksha, the God whom they worship appears before them. They could have a dialogue with that God and ask them for whatever they want or any clarifications they need about their life. It is a great dialogue between man and God. And God may grant them their wish. And in case he is not granting it, he will give them a reason why he is not granting it. So it is a one-to-one relationship between man and God. So he gets what he wants.

So it is no longer dependent on faith. It is a real life experience.

It is a real life experience. It does not depend on your faith.

It shows the change in the relationship between man and God.

Yes. There is a change. Something very epochal is happening here. There is a definite change. God is coming very close to man. And man, too. It is a lost relationship. They were supposed to be very close in the last Golden Age. They are supposed to have walked and talked together, you know. Then, there was a strange alienation between man and God. And it degenerated in subsequent yugas. So now that the Golden Age is back, man and God have to come together. They become friends again. That's it.

I see the veils are beginning to thin between the dimensions and lokas. One question that it brings up for me is the idea of death, because so many people are afraid to die, especially when they are conditioned by beliefs about hell, if they have done something bad, or even believe that they have done something bad, that they will go to hell. What actually happens to people as they make that passage?

What happens is that as people die and they are very scared of hell or of being judged by God, then very often they do not continue their journey. They get stuck in the earth sphere as earthbound spirits. That is an unfortunate thing that is happening. If people of different faiths do the necessary rituals and ceremonies, then it is definitely possible to help them. But more important would be to make them talk to God and realize that God is very friendly and is not going to stand in judgment over them. But this is going to require a shift in man's thinking. I think that's the best way to liberate man. He has to get friendly with his God: otherwise, there is needless trouble.

So the actual passage of death is very beautiful and peaceful?

It's very, very beautiful. The process of dying is a very beautiful process. But for most people, it takes about three days to realize they are dead. Somehow it takes that much time. That's why people have to go through ceremonies to help them realize they are dead and then to prepare them for their journey to meet God. So if that can take place, it is very easy. But if, on the other hand, fear is put into the person, they will hang around. Then, they will have to be helped.

So there are spirit helpers who can assist them to go to the appropriate lokas?

Yes, that's why when people come to us, we work with them to help their ancestors, their parents and grandparents, to be cleared. And once these people move away from the earth sphere, the person can actually feel the liberation, they will feel a lightness. It's not something to be believed in, but it can be experienced.

Bhagavan, what about people who have died? When global enlightenment happens, will they also be . . .

They will be spontaneously enlightened. It's not only for the living, but also for the dead.

So then, they can choose to reincarnate again on this earth or somewhere else?

It's up to them whether they want to reincarnate on the earth sphere or some other sphere or some other planet. It's all up to them. Such is the freedom given to man.

Bhagavan, there are many people who have been longing their whole life for love, who feel like this has eluded them, who are so afraid to love, who are so afraid to receive love. What would you say to people like that?

Yes, I think they will soon be soaked and bathed in love. I think there will soon be spontaneous occurrences of this. Before enlightenment occurs, people will have discovered love, I think. And that will soon be followed by enlightenment itself. And that will be followed by oneness with God. I think that will be the order.

So enlightenment, God-realization, love . . .

Enlightenment, God-realization, love: all these things are going to happen. People won't have to try and get there. These will just spontaneously happen.

I think that's the biggest gift that you are offering, that there is no striving necessary. In fact, the striving itself can be a block, an obstacle to receiving it, because then the mind feels like it can do something.

Like it can do something, yes. The poor mind cannot do anything. It is conflict ridden, it is in opposition with itself, it is repetitive in nature, it is too ancient. So really, it can't do much. It has to realize it is helpless and give up. That's when grace can take over.

You speak about the mind as the ancient mind. What do you imply by that?

By that, I imply that basically, its structure has not changed, that fear is at the core of the human mind. Earlier, it could have been the fear of a tiger or lion; today, it is the fear of the stock market or the fear of losing your job. Then, you were very anxious abut the weather; now, you are anxious about your job or other things. The same craving is there, the same desires are there. The objects of desire have changed, but the desire to be something else is still there. You see, fundamentally, man has not changed. That's why I call the mind very ancient. Only the objects have changed. The objects of craving, the objects of fear, the objects of anxiety: they have changed.

But fundamentally, it is the same old mind, living continuously in fear, living continuously in becoming, moving from where you are to where you want to be. It does not stay put. It is not where it should be. It mainly lives in fear. And basically, there is no change in man. So I do not see any difference between Homo sapiens and Neanderthal man. We have had limited experience of people who have lived earlier, and we see that fundamentally, they are the same.

So when we are enlightened, we can leave this mind behind.

You can leave this mind behind, yes. You can become completely free of the mind. I am talking of a transformation where you become free of the mind. I am not focusing so much on a transformation *within* the mind. That, the psychologists and the philosophers can do. And they are doing a fairly good job. So I don't have to waste time on that. But I am talking of becoming free of the mind itself.

Bhagavan, do you have any plans to travel around the world?

Certainly not in the near future. Maybe sometime. It's very possible. I don't really need to travel. I can do my work from wherever I am.

Do you feel that at some point, your work will be over?

Most certainly, yes. The moment the world is enlightened, my work is over. The moment humanity becomes one humanity, one complete humanity, and all the divisions have ceased, my work is over. I am here to remove all divisions in whatever form they might exist.

So, Bhagavan, would you like to say any final words to readers of this book or to people watching this video?

I would like to tell them that though humanity faces a lot of obstacles, and danger seems to be lurking around the corner, I would like to tell them that redemption is around the corner, that we are going to make it!

Bhagavan, I am so grateful to be in your presence, and to know that this redemption is around the corner. I am sure many, many people around the world echo my sentiments, just to know that there is hope and that there is a plan, that we are entering into a Golden Age, and that the deeksha is possible now, that it can actually transform people's lives so completely and so beautifully in a way that was never possible before. So please accept my heart-felt gratitude.

It has been so nice talking to you.

Thank you. Namaste.

Appendix I
Doorway to Eternity

Note: The following three appendices represent an attempt to link the deeksha phenomenon with ancient calendar systems as well as recent developments in astrophysics, quantum physics, and neuroscience. Some readers may not be interested in science, whereas others may find this overly speculative and not scientific enough. Some may discover errors or inconsistencies in certain aspects of the research. Whatever the case may be, the experience of the deeksha stands by itself, and will work for you regardless of specific beliefs or concepts. Feel free to skip over this section if you wish.

As I researched my previous book, *Doorway to Eternity: A Guide to Planetary Ascension*, I came to some understandings and conclusions about the coming mass enlightenment of humanity, what is known in the New Age movement as the Shift of the Ages. These conclusions are very similar to what Bhagavan has said about the mass enlightenment of humanity by 2012. Here, I summarize some of this research, spanning various ancient calendar systems, mystic prophecies, and visions, as well as some very interesting cosmological and geological findings from recent years.

I will begin with the Mayan calendar, which in recent times has become well-known as a prophetic guide for humanity's evolutionary journey. There have been differing interpretations of this calendar system throughout the years. One of these comes from a Swedish researcher, Carl Johan Calleman, author of *The Mayan Calendar and the Transformation of Consciousness* (www.calleman.com). Grace and I met him when he was in Golden City for the Experience Festival, and became good friends with this wise, warm, and wonderful person.

Calleman provides an interpretation of this calendar that is especially fascinating to me, because it allows us to see the energies of creation at work in linear history. The Mayan understanding of cosmic cycles allowed them to pinpoint future events with a great deal of accuracy. Calleman applies this understanding to these current times, and recognizes Bhagavan as one whose mission is to bring these cycles into fulfillment. He has also met Bhagavan and exchanged ideas with him.

According to Calleman, we are now about halfway through the eighth out of nine cycles of creation, all of which simultaneously end in October 2001. (Please note that this differs from another version of understanding in which the Mayan calendar ends in December 2012. 2012 is thus the beginning of the New Time.) Each time we move into a new creation cycle, evolution speeds up and a greater dispensation of avataric energies becomes available. There is a cosmic order to these creation cycles. Each creation cycle goes through a succession of predictable shifts in energy as it moves toward completion, just as a seed moves through predictable stages as it grows into a tree.

It would take too much space to correlate these cycles with current events in history, but it is fascinating to see how Bhagavan's mission has been following the same patterns of ebb and flow. The Mayans believed that the end of their calendar system would signify the end of linear time, and represent the beginning of great cosmic shift.

Bhagavan's vision fits this timetable perfectly. An avatar descends to earth in response to human need, and in fulfillment of cosmic plan. The synchronicity between the ending of the Mayan calendar and Bhagavan's mission for planetary enlightenment represents the realization of a vast divine destiny, a destiny that goes far beyond planet earth .

Interesting research is being conducted by a group of scientists at the Russian National Academy of Sciences in Siberia, headed by Alexei Dmitriev, Ph.D. Our sun is surrounded by an electromagnetic field, the heliosphere, which creates an egg-shaped envelope around the solar system as it journeys through space. The glowing plasma at the leading edge of this heliosphere, they say, has increased in luminosity by 1,000 percent in the past few years, from 10 Astronomical Units to 100 Astronomical Units! The conclusion they derive is that we are moving into a region of space where the energy is very highly charged.

This highly charged energy is exciting the plasma, which is affecting the radiation within the Sun, which, in turn, is affecting all the planets in our solar system. They predict that this is all working up to a crescendo where there will be a sudden expansion in the "base harmonic frequency" emitted by the sun, which will cause a sudden shift in the consciousness of all life in the solar system!

This highly charged, luminous region of space is variously referred to as, the photon belt, the galactic superwave, and the manasic ring. It is a region of expanded galactic frequencies that many believe will propel us into a higher order of evolution. Once our sun experiences this energy, it is then moved out through the sun's equatorial plane, known as the Ecliptic, and out through interplanetary space, permeating every planet. This, in turn, affects the intricate web of life on a planetary level, creating a quickening of the base harmonic frequency of all matter on earth. This is perhaps the same cosmic mechanism that resulted in spontaneous mass evolution in previous cycles of time. We stand at the edge of that same doorway now.

Perhaps all this is synchronistically aligned with the collective avataric consciousness on earth today, what Sri Aurobindo referred to as the "Supramental Presence," preparing us for the incredible shift to come as we enter the Golden Age. Possibly, the extreme climate changes taking place on earth today are a direct outcome of these interrelated phenomena. Like the golden ball of the deeksha, the Supramental Presence is a highly focused, creative intelligence. It is activating on a solar and planetary level what the golden ball activates on an individual level.

As this Supramental Presence continues to expand, I expect that there will be even bigger changes in the heliosphere, which will create continually bigger shifts within the base harmonic frequency of matter. Sunspot activity has increased dramatically recently, which affects weather patterns, as well as human consciousness. There are well-known cycles of sunspot activity that scientists have been charting for several decades, but sunspot activity of the past few years does not seem to fit into those familiar cycles. If this phenomenally increasing sunspot activity is related to the Supramental Presence on earth, sunspot activity will likely continue to increase in the next few years.

All this is closely aligned with the periodicity of the Mayan creation cycles. The ninth creation cycle begins in February 2011, and ends, along with all the other creation cycles, in October 2011. This signifies another major acceleration in cosmic evolution, culminating in a massive quantum leap. Perhaps this is also the time when astronomers tell us we could be crossing the galactic equator.

The galactic equator is the central plane of the Milky Way galaxy. Although our actual journey through the galaxy takes far longer, from a precessional perspective, we cross this equator every thirteen thousand years or so. Every time we have crossed the galactic equator in the past, geologists tell us, this has been accompanied by major cataclysmic activity. The most recent time this happened coincides with the sinking of the continent of Atlantis.

Geologist Gregg Braden associates this periodicity with the reversal of earth's magnetic poles, while Douglas Vogt and Gary Sultan associate this with a nova effect of the sun, in which a blaze of superionized plasma would be pulsed out throughout the solar system. All this could have a disastrous effect on the earth.

Astrophysicist Paul LaViolette speaks of a "galactic superwave," a pulse that emanates periodically from the center of the Milky Way galaxy. It expands spherically across the galaxy. According to him, our solar system is getting ready to experience the next pulse of this superwave. Could the timing of this be related to the ending of the Mayan Calendar?

LaViolette speaks of what could happen as the superwave interacts with the sun. He says that as the galactic superwave expands simultaneously out through the galaxy, it creates a null point in which magnetic and gravitational fields collapse. As the sun experiences this collapse, it would release gas shells around the sun, resulting in a massive ejection of its corona throughout our solar system. This sudden expansion, followed by a contraction, according to LaViolette, could cause some major cataclysmic activity on earth.

Is this why Bhagavan is so insistent that humanity must be enlightened by 2012? When the nova of the sun happens, it has the potential to extinguish life on earth. It could also propel humanity into an evolutionary leap forward. It all depends on our state of consciousness and the subsequent dimensional space that we occupy. An enlightened humanity could use this opportunity to ride the solar wave into planetary ascension.

Geologist Gregg Braden examines the earth's geological records to see whether we are getting close to what he calls a "zero point." This zero point, he says, is the convergence of two trends currently taking place on earth: a lowering of the intensity of its magnetic fields, and a rise in its base harmonic frequency, as measured by the Schumann resonance. The magnetic field of the earth has been gradually deteriorating in the past few centuries, and Braden expects that at a certain point this deterioration will accelerate suddenly, causing a magnetic polar reversal. This collapse and realignment of the magnetic fields could last three days, he says.

Does the completion of the thirteen thousand–year cycle I referred to earlier coincide with the quantum shift of consciousness expected in 2012? My sense is that the ancient mind that Bhagavan refers to is a subtle electromagnetic field that permeates the body of the earth. As these fields collapse and reorient themselves, so will the ancient mind. It's like punching a reset button. The three days that it takes to reorient these fields could well be the three days that Bhagavan refers to when all humanity will suddenly become enlightened.

I have come to believe that our thirteen thousand–year journey back and forth across the galactic equator also coincides with the Vedic cycle of the yugas. In astronomical terms, it is related to the precession of the equinoxes, which is a twenty-six thousand–year cycle that gives us the astrological ages we are familiar with. Although the yugas are classically understood to be millions of years long, Sri Yukteswar, a disciple of Babaji Mahavatar, introduced a new understanding of these yugas. He refers to the yugas in terms of a cyclical orbit around the hypothetical star, Moolam, every twenty-four thousand years. Although the figures don't match exactly, I personally believe that this could be his way of describing the precessional cycle.

If my understanding is accurate, it means that every time we cross the galactic equator (precessionally speaking) we move from a Kali Yuga into a Satya Yuga. It is an instantaneous transition, like water turning into steam. At a particular temperature, as water is heated, there is a "phase transition," and it suddenly changes state. This phenomenon can be seen throughout nature, and can even be noted in the journey of evolution: witness the "hundredth monkey" phenomenon. Some refer to it as a "quantum shift."

What will this quantum shift look like? I spoke earlier about catastrophic events that accompanied such shifts in the past, and which some scientists and prophets predict could accompany earth's transition in the future. How likely are such scenarios? Carl Johan Calleman believes that we are moving toward a "pole shift of consciousness," which is inevitable as we come to the closure of an entire system of time, and cautions against focusing too much on the geophysical aspects of it. I concur with him, and feel that the likelihood of extreme geological changes will continue to diminish as the morphogenetic field of enlightened consciousness continues to expand. As Sri Aurobindo stated, the Supramental Presence has its own unifying intelligence, and is intent on guiding long cycles of evolution into the fulfillment of a grand cosmic design.

It turns out that Bhagavan's birthday falls on 13 Ahau, which is the last signature of the Mayan galactic calendar, or Tzolkin. This is not an accident. Calleman says that 13 Ahau is the energy at which there are no filters blocking the passage of cosmic light. As all the nine creation cycles move toward this Tzolkin energy, all human beings will come into resonance with this enlightening energy. If Bhagavan's plan succeeds, the ending of the Mayan calendar could be the general timing for moving into the experience of collective enlightenment!

Just as individual enlightenment is both an event and a process, so is collective enlightenment, and our transition into the Golden Age. It is like being born, says Bhagavan. By the time we enter the Golden Age in 2012, much will have changed on the planet. According to Bhagavan, "There will be no more poverty; there will be health and abundance for all; and there will be new forms of education, government, science, and medicine. There will be alternative energy sources, new forms of fuel, and technologies that are earth friendly. There will be more love within the family, including the extended family of nations. This is how you will know that the Golden Age has been born."

Even so, this will only be the beginning. It will not yet be a perfect society. Once the child is born, it still has to grow up. There will still be lots of room for growth and improvement. In generations to come, we will experience far-reaching genetic changes within the human species. The new humans will be androgynous, more translucent, and capable of using far more of the potential of the brain. We will consciously travel in and out of our bodies at will. Reproduction will take place differently than it does today, through a process of cocreative manifestation of intent. And as a species, we will move collectively into more and more profound states of divine oneness.

Chapter 10 of the New Testament book of Revelation says that when the seventh angel blows his trumpet, "time will be no more." The Mayan calendar system echoes this understanding, and gives us a timetable for this event, which is the same timetable that Bhagavan is working with. What does this mean? I believe that they are referring to *linear time*, which has to do with the nature of reality inherent in the duality of the ancient mind. As an enlightened planet, we will move into what we could call *cosmic time*, which would be an entirely different experience.

As more and more of us get enlightened, we will step outside of linear time to dream new dreams; we will walk between the worlds with full awareness; we will birth new realities together; and we will allow the power of new creation to burst forth among us. We have experienced such a small portion of the physical universe, and even the physical universe is such a small aspect of the created universes. Can we imagine what it would be like to walk in the full power of divinity as limitless, multidimensional beings?

Appendix 2

Enlightenment and the Brain: A Scientific Commentary on the Teachings of Sri Bhagavan

By Christian Opitz (christian_mukti@yahoo.de)

The state of enlightenment is associated with a change of brain function in various spiritual traditions. Sri Bhagavan, the founder of the Golden Age Foundation, has now expanded this traditional knowledge about the role of the brain in spiritual transformation. The deeksha, or energy transmission, which lies at the heart of the practical side of his teaching, brings about a permanent change in neurological patterns. His statements about the changes induced in the brain through deeksha can be confirmed with the most advanced findings in physics and neuroscience. Here, I present a comparison between some of Sri Bhagavan's statements and my own findings about the physics and neurophysiology of the brain.

Sri Bhagavan describes a disconnection of activity in the parietal lobes as an essential event in the enlightenment process.

The parietal lobes host what some neuroscientists call the orientation association area (OAA). The function of the OAA is to give us orientation in space. You may take it for granted that you can tie your shoelaces and walk through a door, but this is only possible due to furious neurological activity in the rear part of the parietal lobes. Brain damage to this area makes the smallest tasks, such as grabbing a glass of water, impossible, because the injured brain cannot perceive distinctions among the hand, the glass, and the space in between.

On the physical level, the ability to perceive boundaries and distinctions is essential to our ability to carry out tasks. However, in the human brain, the OAA is chronically overactive. This stimulates the amygdala–hippocampus connection, a pair of brain centers that give a sense of meaning to perceptions registered as important. If the OAA, which creates a perception of distinction and separation to a useful degree, is hyperactive, then the amygdala–hippocampus connection has no choice but to interpret this hyperactivity by assuming that separation has more reality than just on the level of physical objects, such as your hand and a glass.

So a person's conclusion is that he or she is fundamentally, existentially separate from anything else. The sense of self—which the brain creates constantly in reaction to a perception of other than self (the basic premise of object relations theory in developmental psychology)—then seems to be absolutely, distinctly separate from everything else. Neuroscience has shown that in deep meditation or prayer, the OAA in the parietal lobe is temporarily blocked from neurological input. This can give temporary states of vastly expanded consciousness, as the sense of separate self cannot find its usual boundaries and expands to find them. However, this is a temporary experience, dependent on altered brain function; a permanent abiding in oneness consciousness is almost impossible to attain in this way.

This echoes Sri Bhagavan's statement that enlightenment has to be given: It cannot be attained by self-effort. The deekshas seem to induce a process of transformation in the parietal lobes that permanently changes their function to a natural level, where physical boundaries can be perceived but unnatural over-activity ceases. The amygdala–hippocampus would then have no more reason or stimulation to create the sense of an existentially separate self.

Sri Bhagavan says that activation of the frontal lobes is involved in God-realization.

The experience of enlightenment, of nonseparation, does not necessarily coincide with the experience of a living God-presence. In Sri Bhagavan's teaching, more than the deactivation of the overactivity in the parietal lobes is necessary to move from enlightenment to God-realization. He speaks about the activation of the frontal lobes as a necessary neurological change for God to come alive in the consciousness of a person. The frontal lobes are associated with the individual will. Many mystical traditions speak about the merging of the individual will with the will of God as both a doorway to and a result of God-realization.

This, however, cannot happen if the frontal lobes are underactive. It is a universal law that anything incomplete in nature seeks its own completion. My own findings in neurophysiology (which deviate from official, university-sanctioned science) show that the frontal lobes of practically all people are chronically underactive. This means that they simply do not have enough neurotransmitters or electrical energy to function anywhere near the optimum. On a subjective level, this is experienced as weak self-will and a feeling of dullness.

Boredom is possible only with underactive frontal lobes. Dopamine, the essential neurotransmitter for frontal lobe activity, is necessary for feelings of enchantment with life and bliss, which often accompany mystical union with God. Lack of dopamine will increase a person's urge to maintain his or her self-will and not let it merge with a greater reality, because something is felt to be incomplete on the individual level. This is also seen in the process of dying: A person who has experienced a fulfilled life usually has a much easier time making this transition. A person who feels something has been missing in life will often cling to life much more. If the deekshas activate the frontal lobes, this could give completion to the individual will, its fullest flowering. At the full flowering of the individual will, it would naturally merge with the greater reality of God.

From this perspective, a "big ego" is actually a compensation of a weak ego that seeks its own completion. Without full activation of the frontal lobes and dopamine saturation, the ego will never find its own completion and subsequently merge into God. To judge a big ego and fixation on one's individual will as lower consciousness is useless, because a weak self-will has a natural urge to fixate on the individual, no matter what any conscious intentions are. The only solution is change on the physiological level, which liberates the individual will from its struggle against surrendering into a greater reality.

Sri Bhagavan says that enlightenment has to be given: It is a gift of grace.

In recent years, Hartmut Müller, Ph.D., from Germany, has developed a new paradigm of physics called global scaling. This exciting new expansion of quantum physics shows, beyond any doubt, that consciousness is the most fundamental "substance" of the universe and that it contains an original design of everything in the universe, following a mathematical formula.

The distances among planets, stars, and whole galaxies; the distance between electrons and nucleons in every atom; the optimum pH for human blood—all this and everything else in the material universe follows the same mathematical structure. This original design is such that everything operates on the least level of stress and the maximum level of efficiency at all times.

An atom is, at all moments, attuned to the source intelligence via a syntropic field. These syntropic fields allow an atom to always know how to function with the least stress and most efficiency. Human beings seem to be the only manifested forms of creation that have, to some degree, lost their attunement to these syntropic fields of life and unity. Once this loss has produced changes in the brain of an individual, it is extremely difficult for the person to reattune himself or herself with the syntropic fields of unity, because he or she no longer knows what these fields are. So humans create all kinds of mythologies, religions, scientific theories about life, and so on, to fill the void.

A person with an overactive OAA in the parietal lobes and an underactive frontal lobe will seek enlightenment (an experience other than separation). All spiritual striving is part of the problem, because it occurs as a reaction to the loss of attunement with the syntropic fields of unity. If our seeking is based in the problem, it is unlikely that it will end in the solution. But if the attunement to the syntropic fields of unity can simply be given, it is indeed possible that enlightenment can happen for everyone.

The original design of the human brain is to perceive unity as the intrinsic reality of life. This original design is latent: It needs a naturally functioning brain to be anchored in human consciousness. If the deekshas attune the brain of a person to the syntropic fields of optimum brain functioning, the individual consciousness will soon realize its seamlessness, its oneness with all that is.

Sri Bhagavan says that enlightenment is a biological and genetic phenomenon.

Traditional spirituality often assigns a low status to the body. It is often seen as just a vessel for consciousness, a shirt that the soul is wearing. Modern physics shows that Sri Bhagavan's view is much more in alignment with what we know about the nature of matter. Distinct divisions among matter, energy, and spirit are illusory. Based on the brilliant vortex model of the atom, which was formulated by Lord Kelvin in 1867, we can see that every atom has the size of the entire universe, and the material objects we perceive are only the densest aspects of atoms.

Matter is the result of an energetic continuum of vortexes of energy taking on increasing density. As Max Planck described in 1910, in this process of energy condensation, matter fluctuates billions of times per second between being matter and being a formless prematerial energy. From this perspective, it makes sense to assume that spiritual transformation has to be anchored on the physical level. When it reaches the densest level of manifestation, all other levels are automatically taken care of, because matter is not at all devoid of the higher dimensions of creation.

On the contrary, matter appears so dense because it includes all the other levels. So when the material or biological level is enlightened, everything else is included. On the genetic level, it is interesting to note that human DNA is 173 centimeters long, but only 3 centimeters carry active genetic information. Modern biochemistry is puzzled at this seeming wastefulness of nature and calls the inactive parts of the DNA introns, defining them as useless waste material.

But nature does not produce useless material anywhere. Introns are, in my opinion (and again I deviate from official science), equal to the latent spiritual potential of the human being. It is my contention that the deekshas flood the inert parts of the DNA with photons, thus activating them. Photons are nature's bridge between subtle energy and matter. Photonresonance is the process by which information from the subtle realms is distributed from the DNA throughout the cell. The 3 centimeters of usually active DNA material carry information needed for mere survival, but when the rest of the DNA molecule becomes active (able to use photonresonance), the individual can move far beyond mere survival, awakening to his or her full potential.

Sri Bhagavan says that the collective mind, or ancient mind, determines the individual's state of mind.

In the 1950s, Hans Selye, M.D., endocrinologist at the University of Montreal, showed that the brain of every normal person was in a chronic state of survival stress that would be appropriate only in an acutely life-threatening situation. This stress response is something we have adapted to so completely that we do not perceive it as particularly stressful anymore. However, in this stress response state, we are bound to be highly conditioned by our environment and the collective unconscious.

Brain research shows that stress response patterns cause a dominance of high-frequency beta waves in the brain. While in beta, the brain is capable only of primitive stimulus-response patterns that we largely adopt from our environment and the collective human consciousness: Real change is next to impossible. Beta is also the state of the least self-healing ability of the body. Spiritual practice can, to some degree, relax the stress response of the brain and allow more decelerated alpha, theta, and delta waves.

However, research shows that individual spiritual practice is far less effective than a given attunement with syntropic fields of life and unity. At the Tracker School of Tom Brown Jr., a leading expert in wilderness skills, a neuroscientist examined the effects of spending time in a pure wilderness. His findings were stunning: Although it takes a novice usually more than a year of dedicated meditation practice to sustain an alpha state for a few hours, people who never meditated in their lives could sustain deep alpha for hours after only forty-eight hours in pure wilderness.

Because nature is attuned to syntropic fields of life, it will quickly entrain the human brain to its own syntropic fields. It is my contention that in individual practice, too much of the energy with which the seeker practices comes from the ancient mind of struggle and lack. The search is based in the problem, not the solution. This seems to be as close to a scientific validation for the need of grace as there can be.

Conclusion

Many scientists and spiritual leaders have called for a marriage of science and spirituality. Modern science was founded in the seventeenth century as a reaction to centuries of blind faith. For two hundred years, scientists tried to confirm the objectivist-mechanistic worldview of Descartes and Newton. This search finally merged into the staggering discoveries of quantum physics in the early twentieth century, which showed that mystics had, for millennia, described reality quite accurately. What was missing for so many years was a system of spiritual transformation that delivers precise and repeatable results. It is my contention, from scientific investigation, personal experience, and anecdotal evidence, that the work of Sri Bhagavan is the first spiritual system to deliver such results, quite possibly on a global scale.

Appendix 3

The Dark Night of the Soul and Brain Science: A Scientific Commentary on the Transformation Process Through Deeksha

By Christian Opitz (christian_mukti@yahoo.de)

In 1977, Ilya Prigogine was awarded the Nobel Prize in theoretical chemistry for his discovery of dissipative structures. Prigogine described how every natural system grows in a nonlinear way: The organizing structure of a system is at some point no longer useful and has to disintegrate before the new structure can emerge. A prime example of this principle is the transformation of a caterpillar into a butterfly. A caterpillar does not really become a butterfly in the cocoon. Rather, it turns into a seemingly chaotic molecular mesh. Out of this apparent chaos, the structure of the butterfly spontaneously emerges.

Mystics have always been aware of this principle. The dissolution of the current sense of self and God before one can experience the true self and God is a common theme in the spiritual teachings of the ages. The medieval Christian mystic Meister Eckhart expressed this knowing in his famous prayer: "Lord, free me from you so that I can truly find you."

Christian mystics called this passage of losing oneself before finding absolute truth the dark night of the soul. *Dark night* does not necessarily refer to a horrible experience; rather, it means that a person cannot see where he or she is going or how to get there. Although every person and every deeksha is unique, this process seems to be a very common one for those who have received deeksha.

From a scientific point of view, the deeksha is a uniquely effective means of not only inducing the dark night of the soul, but, more important, actually making it fruitful. Many people experience a crisis and loss of identity on their spiritual journey, but until now, few have emerged out of such experiences into full enlightenment. In my opinion, the deeksha process is the first ever means to make this transition possible for all of humanity. Two primary factors make the deeksha process far more effective than anything else to guide people through the dark night of the soul into full enlightenment.

1. The activation of the quiescence and arousal system.

Sri Bhagavan says that everything fully experienced turns into joy. There are two basic systems of awareness in the brain, the quiescence system and the arousal system. When someone can experience something with a fully functional quiescence system, which means total awareness, the arousal system becomes activated and joy is experienced. Thus, Sri Bhagavan's statement is fully supported by neuroscientific insight. This also matches the Taoist teaching that at their end points, yin and yang transform into each other.

However, the normal human brain does not have a functional quiescence system. We therefore tend to recoil from so many of our experiences in life because they do not become joyful. Because the parietal lobes are chronically overactive, the quiescence system of the brain is severely handicapped. Likewise, because of chronic underactivity in the frontal lobes, the arousal system of the brain is equally underactive. This leads to a biological urge to never fully experience anything, thus preventing the transformation of any experience into joy.

Without fully experiencing the inner sense of disorientation and chaos of the dark night phase, one cannot pass through it fully. The caterpillar does not resist its own dissolution and can therefore emerge as the butterfly out of its own destruction. Human consciousness, however, does resist these experiences as long as the brain is functioning the way that has been normal for human beings until now.

Biological urges are simply stronger than conscious intentions. Imagine that someone told you that you would become fully enlightened if you just didn't sleep for six months. There goes your enlightenment! No matter how dedicated you are, the biological urge to sleep will be stronger. Therefore, spiritual practices that are performed while the brain is stuck in the limited patterns of an underactive quiescence–arousal system can give only temporary states of enhanced awareness and joy, which, for most people, cannot lead to a dissolution of the old sense of self and the emergence of enlightenment.

If the brain is biologically wired in a pattern of not experiencing with full awareness, the best intentions to change this will be ineffective. However, a direct attunement to the original design of the brain can effortlessly activate the natural functioning of the quiescence–arousal system. This is what the deekshas seem to do. Then, a person can naturally surrender to whatever his or her experience is, because there is a biological basis for such surrender.

To illustrate the difference in effectiveness between intention-based change and a biological change via direct attunement, let's take a look at strength. Strength is a neurological function, not a quality of muscles. The factors that limit a person's physical strength are neurological inhibitions. A person experiencing an epileptic seizure can have so-called superhuman strength because the neurological inhibitions fall away. These inhibitions affect brain areas other than where the inhibitions that keep a person from being naturally enlightened are located, but otherwise they are the same inhibitions.

The world record for the bench press is 897 pounds. This is the result of an extremely talented athlete working very hard with all his desire and intention to be his strongest. A gorilla shares 99 percent of the genetic makeup of a human being, yet without any intention or training or effort, the average gorilla carries out feats of strength that equal a 4,000-pound bench press!

All that a gorilla does is to be attuned to his natural design. Gorillas don't try to be strong: They just are what they are. A human being disconnected from the original design can never match the natural strength that comes effortlessly to a gorilla. Because the biochemical process of neurological inhibition is the same, whether it's the inhibition of physical strength or of the quiescence–arousal system, this example shows why the deeksha, as a given attunement to our original brain design, is so much more powerful than intention-based efforts.

2. The activation and regeneration of the septum pellucidum.

In the 1950s, neuroscientists discovered that the activation of the septum pellucidum, a brain center right in the middle of the brain, can instantly heal chronic pain, depression, and anxiety; give a sense of peace; and, above all, impart a feeling of joy. However, due to the neurological overactivity in the parietal lobes and the resulting lack of neurological energy for the rest of the brain, the septum pellucidum of almost everyone is chronically underactive.

This actually leads to a shrinking of this important brain center, which, in turn, makes joy and aliveness less and less available to a person. This then activates a person's search for experiences that induce joy, because joy is natural and we are biologically wired to experience it. However, once the septum pellucidum has shrunk, only extreme stimulation can activate it to produce joy.

This is the basis of addictions to drugs: overstimulation of the senses and all things of a *rajasic* or *tamasic* nature. The septum pellucidum is the brain's reward center, and when it is not functioning naturally, we experience reward or joy mostly through unnatural means. Even for people who live a pure way of life, joy is often dependent on conditions.

A common description of the enlightened state is unconditional joy. An enlightened person has a naturally functioning reward center that is always on, not just under certain circumstances. A naturally functioning septum pellucidum makes every experience of life rewarding, no matter what it is. As Sri Bhagavan says, everything fully experienced turns into joy. A healthy septum pellucidum allows us to experience joy in everything, making everything rewarding, including the experience of the dark night.

This makes it possible to actually go through such experiences of inner chaos without a biological urge trying to direct us away from them. For the past several years, I have invented and investigated methods for activating the septum pellucidum. Looking at the brain changes in people who receive the deeksha, I have concluded that the deeksha is by far the most powerful means to activate and regenerate the septum pellucidum. This alone makes the deeksha incredibly effective as a means for inner transformation.

Conclusion

From a scientific point of view, the deeksha is unsurpassed in its effectiveness and logic, because it works according to the natural design of human beings. The old way—trying to transform oneself in the face of biological urges and programming that manifest the experiences of separation and suffering—was never based in natural principles, and therefore worked for few people. If enlightenment is our natural state, as so many mystics have said, then only a natural process will be effective in awakening humanity to it.

Our search for the solution to humanity's suffering must come from a different foundation than the reality of suffering. Working against biological urges with intention-based effort is part of the reality of suffering, not part of its solution. Being given an attunement to our original design through divine grace is the way of nature. All other life forms already participate in this natural way.

I am currently conducting further research into the effects of the deeksha. This includes investigating factors that could make the human brain more receptive to the deeksha. It is an exciting new horizon for science, which might finally bring science and spirituality together in a whole new way, complementing and supporting each other for the sake of humanity.

Recommended Reading

The following books and web sites have been meaningful for me.

Arguelles, Jose. *The Mayan Factor, Surfers of the Zuvuya*

Braden, Gregg. *Awakening to Zero Point, Walking Between the Worlds, The Isaiah Effect.* greggbraden.com

Brown, Jr., Tom. *The Quest, The Vision, Grandfather.* tracker school.com

Caddy, Eileen. *The Spirit of Findhorn.* findhornpress.com/bio-4.htm

Calleman, Carl Johan. *The Mayan Calendar and the Transformation of Consciousness.* calleman.com

Cannon, Delores. *The Convoluted Universe.* www.ozarkmt.com

Capra, Fritjof. *The Turning Point, The Tao of Physics.* ecoliteracy.org/pages/fritjofcapra.html

Carey, Ken. *The Starseed Transmissions, Vision, Return of the Bird Tribes*

Carroll, Lee. *The Indigo Children; Kryon, vols. 1–8.* kryon.com

Castaneda, Carlos. *The Teachings of Don Juan, The Eagle's Gift.* castaneda.com

Chopra, Deepak. *How to Know God, The Return of Merlin.* deepakchopra.com

Clow, Barbara Hand. *The Pleiadian Agenda, Chiron*

Cota-Robles, Patricia. *What on Earth is Going On?* 1spirit. com/eraofpeace

Essene, Virginia. *New Bodies, New Cells, New Life.* www.see-publishing.com

Greene, Brian. *The Elegant Universe*

Hawken, Paul. *The Magic of Findhorn.* www.peace4all.com/html/findhorn.html

Hawkins, David. *Power vs. Force: The Hidden Determinants of Human Behavior*

Hubbard, Barbara Marx. *Emergence: The Shift from Ego to Essence*

Hunt, Valerie. *Infinite Mind: Science of the Human Vibrations of Consciousness*

Hurtak, J. J. *The Keys of Enoch.* keysofenoch.com

Jasmuheen. *Living on Light.* selfempowermentacademy.com

Jenkins, John Major. *Mayan Cosmogenesis 2012.* edj.net/ mc2012/fourahau.html

Kenyon, Tom. *The Hathor Material.* tomkenyon.com

King, Godfrey Ray. *Unveiled Mysteries, The Magic Presence, The I AM Discourses*

LaViolette, Paul. *Earth Under Fire.* etheric.com

MacLean, Dorothy. *To Hear the Angels Sing.* lindisfarne.org

Maharaj, Nisargadatta. *I Am That*

Marciniak, Barbara. *Path of Empowerment, Bringers of the Dawn, Earth.* pleiadians.com

Melchizedek, Drunvalo. *Ancient Secret of the Flower of Life, vols. 1 & 2.* drunvalo.net

Pereira, Patricia. *The Arcturian Star Chronicles.* beyondword. com/books/asc.html

Redfield, James. *The Celestine Prophecy, The Tenth Insight.* celestinevision.com

Roads, Michael. *Talking with Nature, Journey into Nature, Journey into Oneness*

Rother, Steve. *Re-member: A Handbook for Human Evolution, Welcome Home: The New Planet Earth.* lightworker.com

Russell, Peter. *The Global Brain Awakens, A White Hole in Time.* peterussell.com

Satprem. *The Mind of the Cells, Sri Aurobindo and the Adventure of Consciousness*

Sheldrake, Rupert. *A New Science of Life.* sheldrake.org

Sitchin, Zecharia. *The Twelfth Planet.* sitchin.com

Spangler, David. *Revelation: The Birth of a New Age, Reflections on the Christ*

Spaulding, Baird. *Life and Teaching of the Masters of the Far East, vols. 1–6.*

Sri Aurobindo, *The Life Divine, The Future Evolution of Man*

Timms, Moira. *Beyond Prophecies and Predictions.* hoep.org

Tolle, Eckhart. *The Power of Now*

Twyman, James. *Emissary of Light, Secret of the Beloved Disciple.* emissaryoflight.com van Vrekhem, Georges. *Beyond Man: The Life and Work of Sri Aurobindo and the Mother, Patterns of the Present*

Vogt, Douglas, and Sultan, Gary. *Reality Revealed: The Theory of Multidimensional Reality*

Walsch, Neale Donald. *Conversations with God* series. conversationswithgod.org

Ward, Suzanne. *Matthew, Tell Me About Heaven* and *Revelations for a New Era*. matthewbooks.com

Wright, Machaelle Small. *Behaving as if the God in All Life Mattered*. perelandra-ltd.com

Yogananda, Paramahansa. *Autobiography of a Yogi*. yogananda-srf.org

Yukteswar, Sri. *The Holy Science*.

Zukav, Gary. *The Dancing Wu Li Masters, The Seat of the Soul, Soul Stories*. zukav.com

Glossary

Amma—The name popularly used to refer to Sri Padmavati Devi. She is regarded as an incarnation of the Divine Mother, and, along with Bhagavan, her husband, is considered an avatar.

Ancient mind—Rather than having separate, individual minds, Bhagavan says that each of us is simply a channel for this collective, primeval mind, which has existed as a continuously growing *morphogenetic field* since the beginning of human history. It includes all the human tendencies that we generally tend to identify as ours: jealousy, anger, hurt, frustration, lust, happiness, greed, warring, and so on.

Antaryamin—The indwelling presence, or *atman*, known in the West as the *higher self, essence,* or *inner divinity.* This becomes our identity once the illusion of a fixed and separate **self** is dissolved.

Ascended master—One whose physical body has merged with the light body, thereby transcending limitations of space, time, disease, aging, and death.

Ascension—A state of full-body enlightenment wherein the physical body merges with the so-called light body, a state that has been experienced by *ascended masters,* such as Babaji, Ramalinga Swami, St. Germaine, and several others.

Assemblage point—Derived from the teachings of Don Juan, a Yaqui medicine man, it refers to various centers of consciousness in the physical and subtle bodies, which determine our experience of reality. The *deeksha* shifts the assemblage point, so that we can move into a permanent state of altered reality.

Atman—The essential self, the divinity within. It is the individualized aspect of *Brahman*. See also *antaryamin*.

Avatar—A descent of divinity into human form. Each avatar incarnates for a specialized purpose in order to raise humanity to the next level of collective evolution. Einstein was an avatar of physics; Bhagavan is an avatar of enlightenment. We are now entering the age of the *collective avatar*, says Bhagavan, and so this avataric consciousness will flow through a *critical mass* of people, who will then give enlightenment to the rest of the world as we transition into the Golden Age.

Bhagavan—Literally means "bestower of blessings," and is a Hindu term referring to anyone who has realized God. It is also the current legal name of a man in south India who says that he is a technician, specializing in transmitting enlightenment through a neurobiological reorganization of the brain. Along with his wife, Amma, he is considered an avatar.

Brahman—The universal spirit that pervades all creation and exists beyond creation. When individualized through any point of creation, it is known as the *atman*.

Chakra—Literally, "wheel" in Sanskrit. The *kundalini* energy flows through these seven centers of energy along the spine, maintaining the life force of the body. When the chakras are dormant, one lives in separation consciousness. When they are fully activated, one becomes enlightened.

Consciousness scale—David Hawkins, author of the book *Power vs. Force*, used applied kinesiology to devise a scale of consciousness ranging from 0 to 1,000. At the bottom of the scale are states of mind such as guilt, shame, and fear, while the upper end of the scale reflects love, joy, and various levels of enlightenment. Hawkins claims that when a person vibrates on the higher end of this scale, he or she can offset millions of people vibrating at the lower ends of the scale, an assertion that explains how mass enlightenment might be accomplished.

Critical mass—When a certain amount—a critical mass—is achieved, transformation suddenly and irreversibly happens. This could relate to water turning to steam or to the *hundredth monkey phenomenon* or to global enlightenment!

Dark night of the soul (or cloud of unknowing)—A period of time, sometime after enlightenment has taken place, when the personal unconsciousness is emptied out. It can be experienced as an intense emotional dryness, emptiness, and inner struggle; it is what Jesus experienced in the wilderness before the start of his ministry. This process of clearing the unconscious can happen only once the self has dissolved, and is not the same, in Bhagavan's definition, as the periodic slumps that we pass through before enlightenment.

Darshan—A Sanskrit word meaning "interview" or "gathering."

Dasaji—The former name used for the *guides* at Oneness University. The term literally means, "one who serves."

Deeksha—The transfer of energy, directed by Bhagavan, which creates a neurobiological shift in the brain, ultimately leading to enlightenment. Although usually a hands-on experience, the transfer can also take place through a glance, a prayer, or a thought, or simply by being in the presence of someone who is enlightened.

Dimensions—Also known as *lokas*, these are a multitude of worlds, each operating on a different vibrational frequency, within the created universes. The physical world is only one of these. Bhagavan speaks of twenty-one lokas, each associated with a specific chakra (seven within the body, seven below the body, and seven above the body), which incarnated humans are allowed to explore.

Dosha—The ayurvedic system of Indian medicine proposes that the health of the human body has to do with the balancing of three doshas: vata, pitta, and kapha. When these doshas are in balance, the body becomes more receptive to the *deeksha*.

Ego—The Western equivalent of what Bhagavan refers to as the *self* (as distinct from the Self, or Atman).

Enlightenment—A state of consciousness where the *self*, or *ego*, is recognized to be an illusion. When the self dissolves, a new identity emerges, which is the *antaryamin*, or **higher self**. Bhagavan maintains that enlightenment is a neurobiological phenomenon. It cannot be achieved through one's own efforts, any more than a drowning person can pull herself out of the water by her own hair. Rather, it can be given as a gift of grace through a transfer of energy known as the *deeksha*, which reorganizes the brain, thus leading to enlightenment. The first stage of enlightenment is the witness. In later stages, the individual deepens into states of unity consciousness with all creation, and, eventually, with God: I am That. As more and more people become enlightened, says Bhagavan, it will create a *morphogenetic field*, which will ultimately bring about collective enlightenment for all humanity.

Essence—See *antaryamin*.

Galactic equator—The central plane of the Milky Way galaxy. We cross the galactic equator twice in our precessional cycle. We are currently (from 1998 to 2012) experiencing this crossing.

Galactic superwave theory—Proposed by Paul LaViolette, this theory postulates that a massive emanation of energy is pulsed out from our galactic core every thirteen thousand years or so, each pulse lasting several hundred to several thousand years, and due to reach us again shortly.

Golden Age—Bhagavan speaks repeatedly of the current era as an Age of Enlightenment. Also called the Satya Yuga, or "Age of Truth," he says that according to many Hindu scholars, this officially began in 2003, although it may take a few decades for the effects to be fully manifest. The Golden Age is expected to last 1,000 years.

Guides—The teachers, helpers, or deeksha-givers at Oneness University. Formerly known as *dasajis*, they went through years of specialized training with Bhagavan before the public deeksha programs began.

Higher self—See *antaryamin*.

Hundredth monkey theory—A metaphor for the way *morphogenetic fields* function, the story goes that a certain tribe of monkeys were observed on a Japanese island learning to wash sweet potatoes in the river before eating them. As more and more monkeys began to teach each other to do this, something unexpected happened. Suddenly, one day, as a hypothetical hundredth monkey learned this new behavior, every single monkey on the island began to wash their sweet potatoes in the river, and not only that, but every monkey of that species on neighboring islands also began washing their sweet potatoes. A critical mass had been reached in the evolution of that species, which affected the mass consciousness fields of that species, creating an entirely new genetic pathway!

Indigo children—A transitional species of humans who are being born in our midst today, forerunners of an Age of Peace.

Inner divinity—See *antaryamin*.

Kali Yuga—Hindu cosmology speaks of four *yugas*, or ages, which follow each other in linear succession. The darkest of these is the Kali Yuga, and the lightest of these is the **Satya Yuga**. We are currently in a transition from a Kali Yuga to a Satya Yuga.

Kalki—In Hindu mythology, the tenth incarnation of Vishnu, who is predicted to come at the end of the *Kali Yuga* to lead humanity into the *Golden Age*. It is the name formerly applied to *Bhagavan*, until he decided to stop using it due to the controversy it engendered. This is the age of the collective avatar, he maintains, and everybody who is enlightened, and working for the enlightenment of humanity, is a Kalki.

Karma—The law of universal action, which states that we reap what we sow. It is the means whereby a soul gathers experience through its journey of existence.

Kosha—Literally, "body" or "sheath." Five koshas interpenetrate one another in every incarnated human being. These are the *anandamayakosha*, or bliss body; the *vignanamayakosha*, or wisdom body; the *manamayakosha*, or mind body; the *pranamayakosha*, or etheric body; and the *annamayakosha*, or food body, which our senses recognize as the physical body.

Kundalini—The life force energy that runs through channels, or *nadis*, in the spine, known as the *ida, pingala,* and *sushumna*. It passes through seven *chakras*, or centers, in the body as it rises from its dormant position at the bottom of the spine up to the crown of the head, where it meets the descending cosmic energies activated by the *deeksha*, resulting in *enlightenment*.

Lokas—Locations in space and time, existing separately and independently of the physical dimension. Many people, as they go through peak states following their enlightenment, find themselves able to travel in and out of lokas. A shaman can travel through lokas at will. See also *dimensions*.

Morphogenetic fields—According to a theory proposed by Rupert Sheldrake, these "form-generating" fields provide the basis for our memories of the past and possibilities for the future. They permeate the *thought sphere* of any given species, and determine every aspect of its evolution. As illustrated by the *hundredth monkey phenomenon*, a quantum leap in evolution takes place whenever a critical mass within that species has learned a new behavior or achieved a new state of consciousness.. The *akashic* records, said to contain a record of everything that has ever transpired, are a morphogenetic field.

Mukti—Literally, "freedom" in Sanskrit; refers to the freedom from suffering that results from enlightenment.

Nadis—The channels in the spine, and also throughout the body, which carry the **kundalini** energy.

Nagual—A term used by the Yaqui shaman Don Juan to denote the realms of unified consciousness. The laws of the universe operate differently in this realm than in the physical realm.

Oneness University—The location of Bhagavan's training programs in south India, where various programs are offered to the public, including courses in parenting, emotional healing, ayurvedic cleansing, and enlightenment.

Phala deeksha—A specialized deeksha offered at Oneness University, which puts participants into a state where they are able to experience and interact with Amma and Bhagavan in their cosmic bodies. They are then invited to ask for what they desire: better health, enlightenment, more money, improved relationships, and so on.

Photon belt—A metaphysical theory regarding our periodic encounters with a band of high-frequency photons. Such an encounter could result in either cataclysmic destruction or spiritual rebirth—or both. Although this term was first used in science fiction, elements of this theory can be seen reflected in various cosmic phenomena.

Sadhana—A Sanskrit term meaning "spiritual practice."

Samadhi—Unity consciousness. Classically, there are four stages of samadhi in Hindu mysticism. *Savikalpa samadhi* refers to the early peak experiences of oneness with God. As one spends more time in this state, it evolves into *nirvikalpa samadhi*, a relatively nonfunctional state where the person is permanently anchored in oneness. In the third stage, *sahaj samadhi*, the physical body becomes attuned to this oneness to the extent that one is now able to function normally while also holding unity consciousness. In the fourth stage, *soruba samadhi*, which is rare, the entire physical body dissolves into light. This process is also known as *ascension*, and one who has achieved this state is known as an *ascended master*.

Sankalpa—A strong intent, deriving from a recognition of a divinely unfolding plan.

Satya Yuga—In Hindu cosmology, this is the lightest of four yugas, or ages, which follow each other in linear succession. We are currently transitioning from a *Kali Yuga* to a Satya Yuga, which can also be referred to as a *Golden Age*.

Self—When this word is lowercase, it is the ego: an illusory center of identity, which is based in the concept of separation, of existence apart from the whole. When this word is uppercase, it usually refers to the *atman*.

Siddha master—Sanskirt term for **ascended master**.

Soul—Also known as *atman, higher self, antaryamin,* or *essence*, this is a center of identity based in unity consciousness. It is a flow of consciousness revealed as the basis of human identity once the illusory self has been dissolved.

Supramental—A state of unified harmony that exists beyond the mental ego of ordinary human consciousness.

Supramental beings—A future race on earth, perhaps some three hundred years hence, in which an expanded soul consciousness will be fully incarnated within bodies of "true matter," according to Sri Aurobindo.

Supramental consciousness, or **supermind**—A **morphogenetic field** of unity consciousness, as expounded by Sri Aurobindo and the Mother, which was anchored into human collective consciousness in 1956, and will be further activated within each human being in the course of humanity's journey of spiritual evolution.

Supramental descent—The term used by Sri Aurobindo and the Mother to mean the quantum awakening in earth's future. This is a state where the higher spiritual worlds are unified within cellular consciousness, within human bodies as well as within all matter on earth. It would signal the beginning of a new evolution on earth.

Supramental Manifestation—Descent of the supramental presence on earth, thereby lifting the vibrational frequency of all humanity from duality to unity consciousness.

Supramental Presence—As explained by Sri Aurobindo, this is a divine force of unification, operating from beyond the dimensions of space and time, which has been shaping the long journey of cosmic and planetary evolution.

Thought sphere—The sum total of all the thoughts and emotions held within the **ancient mind** of humanity. This will dissolve once mass enlightenment takes place, to be replaced by the **supermind,** an enlightened field of consciousness that will permeate the **morphogenetic fields** of every species on earth!

True matter—A term used by Sri Aurobindo representing the potentiality within matter to come into its divine frequence. Like a caterpillar transferring into a butterfly, our physical bodies are in process of transformation into light bodies, consisting of true matter.

Yugas—The world ages in Hindu reckoning, diminishing from the Satya Yuga, an age of light through the Treta and Dwapara Yugas to the Kali Yuga, an age of darkness. According to some, we are currently about to shift from a Kali Yuga to a Satya Yuga. The "purification" that we are currently undergoing is a necessary aspect of this shift.

Zero point—A term coined by geologist Gregg Braden referring to the convergence of two long-term geological trends, one being the gradual deterioration of earth's electromagnetic fields, the other being the steady increase in its base harmonic frequency. Braden expects that there will be a collective initiation of the planet when this moment arrives. According to John Major Jenkins, the term also refers to a "still point" of infinite creative potential, which will be revealed in the moment of crossing the galactic equator—a reset button for galactic consciousness. It also refers to certain forms of "free energy" technologies.

Worldwide Deeksha Contacts

To explore continually updated articles and links on deeksha and related themes, please refer to my web site, **deekshafire.com**. There are a number of other excellent web sites you may also wish to browse through, including **globaloneness.com, onnessawakening.nl, onenessforall.com, onenessmovement.org, onenessmovementdc.org, ronroth.org, MauiDeeksha.org, Deeksha.com** and **onemovement.org**. The official Oneness University website is **onenessuniversity.org**.

Although a wide range of deeksha courses are being offered worldwide for those seeking more profound states of oneness, the training to become a deeksha giver is currently being offered only in Golden City, South India. Schedules and further information on all these programs can be found on the web sites in the preceding paragraph. It should be noted that the training in India is only for those who are serious about giving deekshas as a soul calling. It is not necessary for those who simply want to receive deekshas.

There is a growing network of people around the world who are empowered to give the deeksha. Many of these can be found through the preceding web sites. Someday soon, we hope to compile one worldwide deeksha-givers list and post it on the World Wide Web!

Because the avataric consciousness knows no boundaries of time, space, or religion, you may also begin to connect with this cosmic energy within your own heart. If you would like to experiment with receiving long-distance deeksha, please "tune in" on the first and third Mondays of each month, between 8:00 and 8:30 P.M. local time wherever you may be.

Find a quiet place, relax, call on your higher self to make the connection, and notice what you experience!

About Kiara and Grace

Kiara Windrider, M.A., is a licensed psychotherapist, spiritual teacher, and author of *Doorway to Eternity: A Guide to Planetary Ascension.* Born and raised in India, he has spent many years studying and practicing in the United States. He first met Bhagavan in August 2003. He met his wife, Grace, shortly before his return to India.

Grace Sears is a Canadian-born mystic and ordained minister. She is the mother of three beautiful children.

Kiara and Grace have both undergone the enlightenment process, including the empowerment to give deeksha, and are both committed to the unity of humankind and our entry into the Golden Age. They have been traveling constantly since receiving their deeksha training and are available to give deekshas, workshops, and lectures worldwide on the themes of planetary healing and awakening.

Your comments are welcome. Kiara can be reached at kiara@deekshafire.com, or through his web site, www.deekshafire.com. Grace can be reached at grace@deekshafire.com.